To B
the Mickey
Mantle of
M.D.'s - Best
Bob 1/1/ 3
R. Kravetz7@
gmail.com

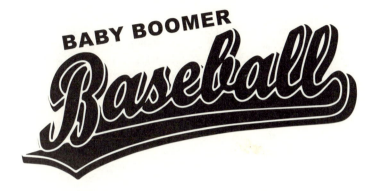

True Stories from the Golden Age of the Game

By
Robert Kravetz

Copyright © 2019 Robert Kravetz.

Cover Illustration by Chris Bonnet

All rights reserved. No part of this book may be used or reproduced by any means, graphic, electronic, or mechanical, including photocopying, recording, taping or by any information storage retrieval system without the written permission of the author except in the case of brief quotations embodied in critical articles and reviews.

This book is a work of non-fiction. Unless otherwise noted, the author and the publisher make no explicit guarantees as to the accuracy of the information contained in this book and in some cases, names of people and places have been altered to protect their privacy.

Archway Publishing books may be ordered through booksellers or by contacting:

Archway Publishing
1663 Liberty Drive
Bloomington, IN 47403
www.archwaypublishing.com
1 (888) 242-5904

Because of the dynamic nature of the Internet, any web addresses or links contained in this book may have changed since publication and may no longer be valid. The views expressed in this work are solely those of the author and do not necessarily reflect the views of the publisher, and the publisher hereby disclaims any responsibility for them.

Any people depicted in stock imagery provided by Getty Images are models, and such images are being used for illustrative purposes only. Certain stock imagery © Getty Images.

ISBN: 978-1-4808-7488-6 (sc)
ISBN: 978-1-4808-7489-3 (e)

Library of Congress Control Number: 2019934403

Printed in the United States of America

Archway Publishing rev. date: 4/10/2019

DEDICATION

This book is dedicated to the Baby Boomer generation of baseball fans who cherish times past and America's pastime.

I am deeply thankful for my family: my soulmate and lovely wife Jill, Adam, Jenny and Nathaniel, Lauren, Ben, Max and Alexander, Maurine and Lee, and Howard.

In remembrance of our most wonderful parents: Marilyn & Bernard Kravetz
Adele & Max Stoler
Vera Kravetz

All profits from **Baby Boomer Baseball** will help support charities such as:

Challenger Baseball (Checks to: Challenger Miracle Field)

CURE (Childhood Cancer Association)

Camp Abilities (Children with visual impairments)

The Gary Carter Foundation (Children and families dealing with autism and other issues)

CONTENTS

Foreword
   by Hall of Famer Gary Carter ix
Introduction xi

Chapter 1	A 1,000-Foot "Tater" (with Paul E. Susman)	1
Chapter 2	Hitting the Ball Squarely	26
Chapter 3	You're on the "Spit List"	30
Chapter 4	A "Real" No-Hitter	32
Chapter 5	To DH or Not to DH? What a Ridiculous Question!	40
Chapter 6	The "Fair" Line	43
Chapter 7	Plays of Fate	50
Chapter 8	Baseball Players Are Superstitious	63
Chapter 9	Nice Guys Finish Last?	66
Chapter 10	"Pitchers Can't Hit"	76
Chapter 11	Pitchers Who Have Won the MVP Award	85
Chapter 12	"If You Don't Believe Me, You Can Look It Up!"	96
Chapter 13	"The Cream Rises"	104
Chapter 14	Other Neat Baseball Expressions	110
Chapter 15	"Real" Hall of Famers	117
Chapter 16	A Clutch Performer	125
Chapter 17	"Good on Paper"	132
Chapter 18	The Greatest Yankees	137

Chapter 19 The Greatest Athlete of the Century............140
Chapter 20 The Next Murderers' Row & the
            Future of Baseball.........................149

Epilogue
    Mickey Mantle: An Appreciation by Scott Pitoniak... 153
Appendix
    Mickey's Phenomenal Career 157
Bibliography...197
Acknowledgements
    "You just don't know"............................. 202
About the Author... 205

FOREWORD

by Hall of Famer Gary Carter

Upon meeting Bob Kravetz, late in October of 1997, I was struck by his true passion for our great American pastime. Bob and I spent part of two days together. He was the volunteer Chairman of the Cancer Action, Inc., Sports Dinner, and I was one of their guest speakers. The other was the great U.S. decathlon champion, Bob Mathias.

We quickly got to know each other, and I was struck by the similarities between us. I also noticed that Bob had a very keen insight about baseball research, which exceeded that of some nationally renowned writers and sportscasters. We chatted about the desire to win in sports and in life. I soon realized that, although Bob's sports career was as an amateur only, he maintained a vigorous pace and drive that he had. There must have been another connection.

At the dinner, I found out that Bob and I had both lost our mothers to cancer when we were very young. We had both learned not only to love life but also to be extremely thankful for what we have. Baseball became a passion of ours at a very tender age.

As I reviewed Bob's manuscript, I knew that it would be another fabulous read. He has the unique ability to conduct great research, combined with writing that has a wide appeal to baseball fans. But even more than his writing, he uses a unique blend of human-interest stories combined with a keen sense of humor which captivates his readers.

Bob constantly supports his community by participating in fundraisers with his first book, *Where Have You Gone Mickey Mantle?*. You are in for a real treat as you read this book.

Gary Carter
2003 Baseball Hall of Fame Inductee
Written in 1997

Robert Kravetz pictured with Gary Carter and a copy of *Where Have You Gone Mickey Mantle?*

INTRODUCTION

"Baseball was, is and always will be to me the best game in the world."
— *Babe Ruth*

This book was written for all those who loved baseball as they were growing up. Baseball has enchanted so many generations of players and fans with its charm and has served as one constant in American existence since the 19th century. Baseball was and is the real American pastime.

Baseball symbolized being an American child, where kids could freely express themselves in a pick-up game on a sandlot diamond and be whomever their hearts desired.

The summer sunshine beat against our brows for eight hours a day every day as we basked in the friendly but meaningful competition. In pursuit of greatness, we practiced and played all that we could on dirt and grass. We used wooden bats. Pitchers hit for themselves. We had memorized the Major League rosters and chosen our favorite players. Mine was Mickey Mantle.

True baseball fans could name the starting lineups from their favorite teams and probably most of the 16 Major League teams. Trades were rare, especially of big-name players. Mickey had to play for the Yankees, Ted for the Red Sox, Stan for the

Cards, Willie for the Giants, "Duke" and then Sandy for the Dodgers, Roberto for the Pirates, and Hank for the Braves. (Until the very end, at least, for Willie, Hank, and the Duke.)

The summer marathon games started early, as fields were tough to find. A fist fight for field rights was not out of the question. We would leave our houses on our bikes and reach the field by eight o'clock in the morning with a mitt in hand and a dime or maybe 50 cents in our pockets. Lunch hour might be at home, but someone always stayed at the field to protect your rights. One of us might ride to the corner store for pop and candy for lunch or ice cream sandwiches.

We would often play another pick-up game after dinner, sometimes with different players and usually closer to our neighborhood. We would do anything for a few more swings per day.

The choosing of sides was a unique experience in itself. Usually, we would try to "cap" the bat. One by one, we would place a hand on the bat. Whoever reached the top would win the rights to first pick. Anyone whose final move was a two-fingered scissors insertion would have to take the bat with those two fingers and twirl it around his head without dropping it.

A few lads were lucky and owned a bat, which had to be shared. But beware: the batter better be facing the trademark so that he didn't crack this valuable item. A brand-new ball was real a novelty. We would often use the same baseball until we had knocked the cover off of it. Otherwise, we repaired the baseballs with black shiny electrician's tape and the bats with a small finishing nail and black tape. The sticky black tape had the effect of too much pine tar. Albeit George Brett didn't mind the overuse of pine tar, but Billy Martin did!

Boys learned the art of fending for themselves without

parents hanging over their shoulders. We settled our own arguments as we developed our baseball skills. We artfully learned the intricacies of this beautifully simplistic game. Team pressure of winning dictated when to go for the fences or when to go for just a base hit. It became evident who was good in the clutch and who was a choke artist. We knew who had a great winning attitude and never gave up – those had a real love for our most cherished game.

Baseball: that beautiful *crack* of the bat and the snare of a screeching line drive, with two outs and the go-ahead runs on base. Children playing as children should. Inherently, we understood that Little League was just a show for the parents. Sandlot games against our close group of friends and peers was the real game, where we established our place in society.

When I was five years old, I vividly remember watching our black-and-white Magnavox TV, and seeing Willie Mays making his great catch of the ball Cleveland's Vic Wertz hit during the 1954 World Series. At that exact moment, a benchmark of greatness was etched into my young impressionable mind.

My beloved father and unparalleled mentor, Bernie, stood up off the couch. "Never ever forget that catch," he said. "They will call that the best catch in history, ever." Thank you, Dad.

From that point on, I no longer merely watched men playing a boy's game. I had a yardstick by which to measure a superb level of talent.

"Some psychologists say that a child's personality is formed by the age of six," Marvin Miller, the first Executive Director of the Major League Baseball Players Association, said in his book *A Whole Different Ball Game*. "It's difficult, perhaps impossible, to unravel the separate threads which make up your life and from them determine a credible cause-and-effect that explains how you become the person you are."

Willie provided one such event. Mickey provided a million more throughout the 1950s and '60s.

*

French-American historian Jacques Barzun said, "Whoever wants to know the heart and mind of America had better learn baseball, the rules and realities of the game…"

But baseball is about more than the rules. Baseball is the warp and the woof of American fabric but working with human clay. It is the stuff of which American heroes -- of war and of peace – are made.

Growing up, I emulated my father. He was one of the hundreds of thousands of World War II GI heroes who returned home safely, ready to celebrate the triumph over oppression and terror.

Our fathers were American heroes and the heads of strong family units, managers of a cohesive, trusting, confident team. With Americans safe after World War II, it was time to play. Little boys and big ones, too, transferred their heroes from the battlefield to the baseball diamond. Instead of MacArthur and Eisenhower, we praised "The Splendid Splinter" and The Yankee Clipper."

American baseball flourished in peacetime since the end of the Civil War. With peace after World War II and balance finally restored, baseball was now ready to return to normalcy. Returning to the major league baseball diamonds were Ted Williams, Joe DiMaggio, Bob Feller, Hank Greenberg, Luke Appling, Phil Rizzuto, Yogi Berra, Tommy Henrich, Joe Collins, Charlie Gehringer, Gene Woodling, Vern Stephens, and others.

My baseball hero – and the hero for about 20 to 40 million

other boys – was Mickey Mantle. When I was seven years old, I would rip open the morning newspaper to see if Mickey had beat out Al Kaline for the runs batted in (RBI) part of the Triple Crown and Ted Williams for the batting average honors. Both pieces were close races. Mickey prevailed in 1956 and became the only MLB Triple Crown winner ever to achieve more than 50 home runs with this extraordinary feat.

The institution of baseball was stabilized in 1920, just after the end of the Federal League and the scandal of the 1919 "Black Sox." Just after World War I, a three-man National Commission elected the first commissioner, for no less than a seven-year term. Judge Kenesaw Mountain Landis was a Czar-like figure. Landis was a judge of the United States District Court as arbitrator, a one-man court of last resort. *The New York Times* read: "Baseball Peace Declared; Landis Declared Dictator."

Landis's job was to protect the institution and prestige of baseball, regardless of his style. Although the players had formed their own unions, Landis kept the reserve clause in force.

Baseball became the official American pastime with the establishment of the National League of Professional Baseball Clubs. The League was created in the spring of 1876, the same year that Chief Sitting Bull swept Lt. Col. George A. Custer at Little Bighorn Field. This was the last significant sweep by the Indian's for about 100 years!

By 1879, the National League's eight teams had developed a compact. At the end of the season, each team would "reserve" five players, making them off limits to any other team. Soon the reserve clause grew to encompass all players. Now, the owners could easily hold down players' salaries and cut expenses that would have enhanced playing conditions.

The Brotherhood of Professional Baseball Players, a union, was formed in 1885. Together, the players protested playing conditions and meager salaries. John Montgomery Ward was the star infielder for the New York Giants. Ward led the Giants to championship victories in 1888 and 1889, hitting .379 and .417 and stealing 17 bases in what is now known as the World Series. Ward, also a law school graduate, became the head of the Brotherhood and said, "Players have been bought, sold, and exchanged as though they were sheep instead of American citizens." Interestingly, it was Ward who first claimed that players were ready to strike over "oppressive" conditions and were treated like slaves, not the honorable Curt Flood. Some of Ward's contemporaries had fought in the Civil War and lived during Lincoln's Emancipation Proclamation of 1863. As we see, the battle between the aristocracy and the bourgeois has very deep roots.

But clearly it was not Commissioner Landis who was the savior of Baseball after it suffered a terrible black scar in 1919; it was the enormously talented and spirited George Herman "Babe" Ruth. Babe was his own man. When Landis proclaimed that Ruth and his gang could not barnstorm after the season anymore, where players made excellent money. Ruth told Landis to "go jump in a lake."

Babe Ruth, "The Bambino," was the new ambassador and introduced the weapon called the home run. It was a great fit for America. The United States had recently played a leading role in settling the affairs of the world and was unified in rejoicing. With this came the gluttony of the "Roaring Twenties". Our heroes moved from Europe to Hoboken. This new vibrant "Big Bang" style of play stood for expression of freedom, greatness, and grandeur. Ruth remodeled baseball like the allies remodeled democratic rule. Ruth was a great salesman, who captured the imagination of the American public. He was the "Sultan of Swat" and the King of the American people.

From Lincoln's triumph of restoring our nation as one, past the 1,000 days of John F. Kennedy's presidency, the establishment of baseball ran fairly smoothly. It had a low spot during World War I, especially in 1919. For 100 years, our society was unified in principle, with very few changes. In war, we learned how to love our fellow Americans.

Following the lesson of camaraderie in war, a change which was about a century overdue, was to happen in 1946. Branch Rickey had the *chutzpah* to hire Jackie Robinson to play for the Montreal Royals. In 1947, Robinson was promoted to the Dodgers and broke the official "color barrier" on April 15, Opening Day. A number of people of color had played in the major leagues before, here and there. But this monumental day marked a crucial and much-needed shift in baseball and all professional sports. Soon thereafter, Robinson would team up with Larry Doby, Minnie Minoso, Roy Campanella, Don Newcombe, Luke Easter, and the unparalleled Satchel Paige to fight a different kind of war. This battle for equality, for people of color, was and still is at least as important to our society internally as all wars overseas have been.

Ebbets Field, home of the Brooklyn Dodgers, was a "thing of beauty." The ballpark and its patrons characterized what the United States was all about. This cozy shrine nested their fans. Ebbets Field was the "melting pot," where all races cheered, hoped, and prayed together that this would finally be the year. Each spring brought eternal life and hope. Together, Dodgers fans "waited 'til next year," until 1955 finally rolled around.

The baseball field is where all socioeconomic improprieties were erased by talent alone. Women and men alike cheered when sport was for sport alone, a far cry from bonus babies and billionaires of today. How can anyone be worth more than $30 million a year for their services? Players of the Baby Boomer generation played for the love of the game. We would have paid to play this cherished game.

Before the reserve clause was dissolved, an establishment of absolute tyranny presided over the players with virtually no recourse available, except quitting. The reserve clause held up with only a few skirmishes. In 1947, Danny Gardella sued Major League Baseball over the reserve clause. Gardella won the first round in court and MLB quickly settled out of court. In 1953, George Toolson sued the league for antitrust laws. The Supreme Court quickly upheld the 1922 decision that antitrust laws did not cover Major League Baseball. "Toolson," Miller wrote, "was stuck in a Yankee organization with a well-stocked team."

Players could essentially sign their contracts or quit playing. If you were a true superstar, you could hold out. Koufax and Drysdale held out together and won the battle. Yogi Berra delayed some of his contract signing as did Joe DiMaggio. After the 1956 season when Mickey won the coveted Triple Crown, he wanted a raise that would double his salary and bring him up to about $75,000. Mickey sent his contract back unsigned. Weiss, the Yankee owner, threatened him with a detective's report that would hurt his image, not to mention his marriage to Merlyn. In 1957, Mickey hit for a .357 batting average with 34 home runs (HRs) and 94 RBIs and led the league in walks and runs. The Yankees also won the American League pennant, which meant another extra payday for the Yankee team and front office. Weiss wanted Mickey to actually take a pay cut based on not winning the Triple Crown again.

The press also supported the hard-nosed negotiations of

the owners to stay in their good graces, protecting their access to the press boxes and their jobs. When DiMaggio had his first big season in 1937, with 46 HRs, 167 RBIs, and a .346 average, he wanted $40,000 for 1938. The press got on his case for not accepting $25,000. DiMaggio was fighting the owners, the press and most importantly, his public image.

Owners had tremendous power for generations. In 1933, the great Jimmy Foxx won the Triple Crown and owner Connie Mack wanted to reduce his salary from $16,670 to $12,000. Foxx hit only 48 homers, down from 58. In 1934, Lou Gehrig had a fabulous year with 49 HRs, 165 RBIs, and a .363 BA. He had to struggle to stay at $23,000. In 1938, Hank Greenberg hit 58 home runs, an amazing year for any generation, and had to fight like a dog for a $5,000 raise bringing him up to $40,000.

After World War II, there was continuity in America. The reserve clause lasted for about 100 years. One more bureaucratic commissioner that supported the owners followed another. Joe DiMaggio and Ted Williams replaced the icons of Babe Ruth and Lou Gehrig. Mickey replaced "Joltin' Joe." The Dodgers kept waiting until next year, the Red Sox were cursed, and the Washington Senators were true to their reputation: "First in war, first in peace, and last in the American League."

*

By the 1960s, the times, as Bob Dylan sang, were "a-changin'."

The Baby Boomer generation, like all other generations, had seminal events that took place in our formative years. Who cannot recall those monumental days? The day President Kennedy was shot shattered our confidence in goodness of society and trust in mankind. The trust that was crushed on November 22, 1963, followed by a week of mourning, has never been fully restored. JFK stood for hope for a better future and a New Frontier of technological advances that reached for the moon. He had won the Presidency against all odds, as he was the first Catholic president and the youngest, too.

Around the time Kennedy was running for office, I was racing out of Hosea Rogers School in eighth grade, breathlessly holding my transistor radio to my ear. Much to my chagrin, I heard the grounder hit by Bill Virdon that hit Tony Kubek in the "Adam's Apple" in Game Seven of the 1960 World Series. That was a wonderful seven-game battle where the Yankees slaughtered the Pirates with hits and runs, only to lose the war.

When I first heard Kubek going down, I told myself that that was only one individual play in this crucial winner-takes-all game. But I sensed that it was a miserable "play of fate," just like when I heard Sandy Amoros' sliding catch of Yogi Berra's slicing left-field shot in 1955. Why did this happen again in Pittsburgh in 1960? I have only somewhat recovered from losing JFK. But I don't think I'll ever get over the crippling blow of 1960! (Mickey might not have, either. He cried all the way home on the plane.)

From the owner's point of view, the next earth-shattering event took place with the arrival of Mr. Marvin Miller as the Executive Director of the Major League Baseball Players Association (MLBPA) from 1966 to 1982. Miller was born in 1917, grew up on Flatbush Avenue and rooted for "Dem Bums." He graduated from New York University with a BA in Economics at 19 years old.

When he was working for the New York City Welfare Department, Miller joined his first union and sat on his local's first grievance committee. Soon after World War II broke out, he joined the National Labor Relations Board. It was there that he trained in the art of arbitration, dealing with local disputes. In 1950, he joined the United Steelworkers and headed up their Human Relations Research Committee. In 1966, Miller was elected as the Executive Director of the MLBPA. Although he started out in a major slump due to the new mistrust of authority based on the times, he ended up with as much power off the field as Babe Ruth had between the fair lines. In fewer than ten years, Miller would take baseball down a path of unalterable change. Miller, along with arbitrator Peter Seitz, overturned baseball's structure for the first time since Little Big Horn!

At first, Miller visited each team's camp, but players just wouldn't listen or trust him based on Miller being an authoritarian figure. Back then, the reserve clause was still etched in stone. Miller spoke of increasing salaries and benefits. Why waste time with an idea that wasn't plausible? Furthermore, the players' own government had lied about the severity of the war in Vietnam. Miller was trying to govern their union. (Nixon ultimately prolonged the war for an extra seven years, and the short-memory public and press praised him posthumously.)

The year 1969 was a very exciting year for breakthroughs. Neil Armstrong and Buzz Aldrin walked on the moon in July, and a far-reaching vision of John F. Kennedy's became a reality.

At the same time, the "Amazing Mets," as Casey Stengel called them, were starting to heat up. Tom Seaver went on a tear, leading them to a pennant and into the World Series against the Mighty Orioles. It was David and Goliath. Most everyone predicted a sweep by the Orioles including Frank Robinson. The Mets upset the Orioles in five games, a miracle happened. That year, the brash, flamboyant, anti-establishment quarterback Joe "Willie" Namath of the AFL made good on his promise to the world by beating the Baltimore Colts, proving to the all-mighty NFL that he was king.

In the late winter of '69, just before these monumental events happened, Marvin Miller was still groping for a win. He desperately needed a win. He boldly suggested that players not sign their contracts until a benefit package was added. His boldness exemplified the attitude that had been nurtured and evolved in the hearts and minds of the youth of the sixties. But still he could not get his first win. Miller, in his own words, needed "a lever of some major proportions to effect change."

Coincidentally, Mickey Mantle was his trump card. Through Steve Hamilton, the player representative of the Yankees, Miller quietly found out that Mickey was going to retire. Miller begged for a meeting with Mickey. He also begged Mickey not to mention his retirement and asked Mickey for his solemn support.

Mickey asked the appropriate question based on the reserve clause, "What good would it do for the players?" Miller convinced Mickey that it would do a great deal for the players. Little did Miller know how prophetic he was until December 23, 1975.

Mickey was true to his word. He issued a statement that he would not sign his 1969 contract until the owners included a benefits package. The first explosion of this new war erupted. Most players sided with the great Mickey Mantle, and Miller had his first Major League win, a near no-hitter. After the owners relented, Mickey made it known publicly that he could no longer play efficiently (taking an extra base, going from first to third on a hit, and batting left-handed with power due to his completely incapacitated right knee). Immediately, Mickey retired. One can only imagine what course of events would have taken place without Mickey's support. Miller would have been stranded in the on-deck circle, as the game, season, and era ended!

Another event along the same lines of change followed in 1972. Miller had the players hold out for an increase of $500,000 in their benefit package. The MLBPA voted 663 – 10 in favor of a strike. This tally benchmarked a maturation of a thought process and a revolutionary mindset. The quiet revolution was on. The lines of the next "Civil War" were drawn. The new weapons were updated to assembling, striking, holding-out, lockouts, negotiating and courts of law. The players agreed to revolt against the owners together, unlike the brave Curt Flood. Baseball again paralleled American society, going from Danny Gardella's bombshell that was quickly smothered to the era of an eminent explosion. America's pulse of instability ran wild during this era, going from a potential nuclear incident at the Bay of Pigs to unpredictable guerrilla warfare in Vietnam.

Something else happened when Mickey retired. No longer was there a true superstar and real icon in the game. Willie Mays was old, and Sandy Koufax had retired. So many stars, not superstars, raced into the spotlight to fill the vacancy. Who would rule? Would it be a prolific singles hitter like Pete Rose, a slugger like Reggie Jackson, an all-around player like Hank Aaron or Johnny Bench, or a pitcher like Catfish Hunter?

Jim "Catfish" Hunter was not the first true free agent based on breaking the reserve clause as we know it today. Charley Finley, the flamboyant owner of the Oakland A's, breached Hunter's contract. Finley was supposed to make a deposit from Hunter's paycheck into a named annuity fund every two weeks. Finley reneged for the entire 1974 season. According to Hunter's contract, Finley had ten days to respond to the violation that was put into writing by Hunter and

Marvin Miller. Finley blew it off, displaying his 100-year-old feudalistic attitude.

Peter M. Seitz was the arbitrator who upheld Hunter's right to become a free agent. Hunter was a man of principle and signed with the Yankees on New Year's Eve of 1974 for $3.5 million, agreeing on the back of a paper napkin and with a handshake.

Of supreme importance was the fact that Peter Seitz had rendered his legal opinion as the arbitrator in the National Basketball Association vs. the NBA Players Association. The California Court of Appeals gave Rick Barry the right to sign with the Oakland Oaks of the ABA, after "playing out his option" with the San Francisco Warriors. The NBA Uniform Player Contract was nearly the identical language as Major League Baseball's. That opinion had set a new precedent.

Seitz soon interpreted the language contained in the contracts of pitchers Andy Messersmith and Dave McNally. Messersmith had not signed a contract when Miller approached him. McNally was going to retire. Miller begged him to pitch one more year without signing a contract. Both completed a year of service without signing a contract. Peter Seitz rendered his legal opinion that both had "played out their option."

Now, for the first time since Little Big Horn, the MLBPA had its house in order and the establishment had been impeached. The owners tried desperately to stop the devastation with a few skirmishes of lockouts. Even today, Marvin Miller has not yet been enshrined into the Baseball Hall of Fame. But the balance of power had turned 180 degrees.

*

Ask not what you can do for the game of baseball. Ask how much you can siphon off the game.

Money became the king of our society and of baseball, too. Statistics, charts, and graphs for each pitch on the field have become as prevalent as MBAs in the boardroom – both too often lacking in genuine application.

Catchers are no longer allowed to communicate with the pitcher directly, their comrades on the mound. Catchers are like quarterbacks in football, the generals of the field. Now, they are paid to be puppets and look into the dugout after every pitch, because Big Brother knows better and is paying the bill. Can you imagine Yogi and Whitey, or Thurman and Catfish being instructed to look in the dugout between pitches? How ludicrous!

The real shame of the matter is that it is no longer okay for battery mates to work together without interference, like parents in Little League. American baseball traditions that had flourished since the end of the Civil War were built on the principles of sandlot ball, not Little League.

Ancient Greece had its Olympiad, Rome had its Colosseum, and America's Field of Dreams was once all grass and dirt. Our beloved past diamonds linked our rich heritage of being an agrarian society.

Now, we have plasticky Astroturf and green concrete that produces 99 percent true hops and doesn't teach kids to charge the ball. Singles roll for triples, and shortstops can bounce the ball to first base. It goes against the natural beauty of the game and the rich tradition of our great American pastime. Let's play two on dirt and grass in natural daylight.

1

A 1,000-FOOT "TATER" (WITH PAUL E. SUSMAN)

When we were kids, we played baseball – and later, softball – any chance that we got. Diamonds were tough to come by and sometimes makeshift.

The diamond at Pardee Road wasn't too bad. During a softball scrimmage, I ripped a good shot over the left fielder's head. It landed in a cabbage patch. The Nuns who occupied the adjacent farmhouse helped us retrieve the ball with wide smiles on their faces.

For the next inning, I was playing left field. My friend Garry hit an explosive home run. The ball sailed over my head, over the cabbage patch, and into the potatoes. As I ran to retrieve the ball, I asked the Nun where it had landed. She pointed and said, "Right over there. It hit that long potato."

At the end of the 1997 season, Mark McGwire, who had apparently bulked up enormously by using the Nautilus or a rigorous regimen of weight-lifting, swung at a "rabbit" ball and hit a spinning "pop fly" that just kept carrying and landed 414 feet away. It barely cleared some stumpy center-field fence. This was McGwire's fifty- eighth homer of the season. With this, he tied great sluggers Hank Greenberg and the mighty Jimmy Foxx. The great "Bambino" and the *real* Home Run King, Roger Maris, were in his sights for the future. McGwire had recently surpassed the incomparable Mickey Mantle.

On May 3, 1998, the *Chicago Sun-Times* reported that McGwire was taking creatine to build muscle mass. He started that campaign on a pace like never before. He hit number 40 on July 12, 1998, just after the All-Star break. In August, *The New York Times* reported that McGwire was taking an over-the-counter substance called androstenedione, which he claimed to stop taking during the '99 home run circus. The drug is banned by the NFL, the NCAA, and the Olympic Committee, but it wasn't banned by MLB at that time. McGwire hit 55 homers by the end of August, faster than anyone in history. On Labor Day, September 6, McGwire tied Roger Maris with number 61. On September 9, 1998, he did the unbelievable. He reached number 62 as the whole world watched. Big Mac finished with 70 round-trippers. "Slammin' Sammy" Sosa hit 66, after having a previous high of 40. The race was great for creating baseball excitement and restoring fans.

In 1998, baseball was also blessed with the Yankees' David Wells pitching a perfect game, Kerry Wood's 20-strikeout shutout, the tie-breaker game for National League wild card race, and the Cubs beating the Giants in the 163rd regular season game. Roger Clemens's won the Cy Young Award as well as the Pitching Triple Crown for the second year in a row, which later brought national attention of enhanced results. Cal Ripken, Jr., willingly put an end to "The Streak" and

Juan González's MVP year, and an incredible tally of home runs allowed the gullible fans to be excited. Steven Spielberg could not have written a better script. In 1999, the ludicrous frequency of home runs continued with McGwire hitting a mere 65 and Sosa 63. Sosa hit 66-63-50-64 starting in 1998, which was absurd.

In 2001, Barry Bonds hit a record 73 home runs. He had never hit 50 homers in one year in his entire career. He averaged 27.5 for his first eight years, and averaged 32 for his first 16 years, and never hit one 500-foot shot. But as megasalaries went up, homers did, too. Barry ended up with 762 tainted homers.

But hold on: before comparing McGwire, Sosa, and Bonds, who were obviously the premier sluggers of their generation or today's sluggers Judge and Stanton to Mickey Mantle, one needs to understand what hitting homers since late 1970s really means.

On April 12, 2000, Carol Slezak of the *Chicago Sun-Times* reported, "This year's Bud Selig signature baseball, used by both leagues, has even a harder slicker cover than last seasons. The better to hit home runs with." Furthermore, according to the University of Rhode Island Study, the inner core, "the pill" of the 1995 and 2000 baseballs, was much more resilient and bounced one-third higher than the older balls. This was yet another iteration of the creation of home runs, as we will examine. Without a doubt, Mickey Mantle was the benchmark in terms of power and flight, for all to be measured against.

Since free agency, the economic state of baseball has been in a tizzy. Even George Steinbrenner, the late Principal Owner of the New York Yankees, said he needed three million fans a year to compete with the Dodgers and Orioles. The 1998 Yankees came close to three million fans and got Roger Clemens to boot. In 2004, the Yankees drew nearly four million fans.

But the largest blow to Major League Baseball was the 1994 strike. Unfathomable was missing the World Series! The fans' morale and excitement were at an all-time low. Undoubtedly, the owners asked, "How do we get are fans back?" The answer? More home runs. So, they juiced up the ball like never before, moved the fences in, watered down the pitching through expansion, and shrunk the size of the strike zone to the equivalent of the size of a shoe box, along with various other tricks like performance-enhancing drugs (PEDs).

Another gimmick is the computer estimate of the obstructed home run. To keep attendance high, incredibly exaggerated distances are alleged with no basis in fact or science. Most of today's home runs are dropping. Mark McGwire's could never travel the distances guessed. For example, McGwire's best shot went an alleged 545 feet in St. Louis and cleared the center-field wall at 402 feet. It then hit the green backdrop as it was coming down off the facing of the upper deck -- a heck of a shot even with a juiced-up ball. The distance was an estimate by opinions in the press box. In reality, it went between 500 and 545 feet. Mantle had several blasts at Comiskey Park, Tiger's Briggs Stadium, and old Yankee Stadium that left walls at points of 420, 415, and 402 drilling the upper deck. These shots were much higher than McGwire's as they were still raising at heights of eighty to 118 feet.

McGwire hit long home runs that peaked at the two-thirds range of flight, if unobstructed, then dropped down. That is the ball's natural flight for virtually everyone who has ever played our great national pastime. However, Mickey Mantle was the exception. Often, his prodigious smashes defied the normal pattern and kept rising further out and then ricochet off a structure or dropped. Bonds had maybe reached 500 feet a few times, even with his magic cream! These line drives by Mantle and others topped the alleged 545 foot shot of McGwire's and had to go a minimum of 550 feet, with a softer ball, just by doing the physics and math.

What would McGwire do in old Yankee Stadium? Mickey had the challenge of having the base of the left-center-field wall 461 feet away. The stands then were 31 feet high, at their lowest point. The extreme corner of left-center was nearly 475 feet away. His line drives had to travel 500 feet to clear the wall. Mickey cleared the wall numerous times. Another premier slugger of that generation, Moose Skowron also accomplished this rear feat in 1961. What a remarkable year it was, the best real home run chase ever!

Pristine Yankee Stadium housed the monuments of Lou Gehrig, Miller Huggins and Babe Ruth on the playing field, some 463 feet from home plate. Joe DiMaggio, the "Yankee Clipper," and later Mickey would sail around the monuments and catch fly balls. Yankees catcher Ken Slater, who played with Phil Linz, Joe Pepitone, and Tom Tresh, describes that it was so deep that you could see a haze when looking back towards home plate."

Whitey Ford used to count 450-foot shots that Mickey walloped for outs. In Whitey's most conservative estimates of 1961, he said that Mickey had at least 50 shots that were caught for outs. He also had 54 that were not caught that year. The fact is that Mickey lost 250 to 300 career home runs, as a very conservative estimate. In addition, as Phil Rizzuto and others had noted, "In Mickey's era the wind almost always blew in against the hitter. After that time the wind blew out towards right."

Mickey's former teammate-turned-announcer Tony

Kubek claimed in some years, "Mickey lost at least 25 home runs on balls hit 420 – 450 feet or so, that were all caught for outs."

Johnny Blanchard clearly recalled a doubleheader in 1962, where Mantle blasted seven 440-foot shots to straight away center field, which were all long outs. Blanchard also stated that in the magical season of 1961, Mickey lost 50 balls that were hit 420 feet or more for outs.

Mickey started the 1961 season with an inauspicious debut, going hitless in his first two games. But in the third game, on the first pitch by Kansas City starter Jerry Walker, Mickey slammed yet another long ball batting lefty, off the third-deck facade in right field. This towering drive opened the gate for the start of this supreme season. This was also an un-juiced ball -- something that would change in 1977. In 1961, Mickey's 54 home runs plus today's 50 sure shots that were caught for outs is an astounding 104 homers in my book!

While playing in old Baltimore Memorial Stadium in 1955, before they moved the center-field fence in quite a bit, Mickey hit another exceptional drive of 480 feet. Remarkably, Chuck Diering was playing out in "no-man's land," plunged headlong into a hedge, and caught it for an out.

Other ballparks were just as difficult to drive the ball out of. Cleveland's Memorial Stadium, which was on the edge of windy Lake Erie, was 470 feet to center field during Mickey's era. Mickey hit three unsurpassed upper-deck shots, which all had to be in the 500-foot range. The wind also whipped in off the lake. Nobody ever hit one in the bleachers in a regular game, but Mickey did in batting practice.

For the record, Shibe Park in Philadelphia was 468 feet in center and the Polo Grounds in New York was 480 to 505 feet in center field at times. But the ultimate distance was in the first World Series in 1903, where the Giants' center-field fence was 626 feet and the ball was a "rag-sock."

Occurring from around 1900 to 1919, the "dead-ball era" was characterized by low-scoring games and few home runs. Then Babe Ruth emerged as the league's power hitter, just after the scandal surrounding the 1919 World Series. With his colossal "Big Bang" style of play, he overshadowed the huge stars, mainly Honus Wagner, Ty Cobb, pitcher Cy Young, and manager Muggsy John McGraw, "the Napoleonic genius" who dominated the dead-ball era. The ball itself was not changed until 1926.

Ruth had enormous power and talent and was about to exhilarate the public with his majestic home runs and his boyish exuberance for life. The Babe set another new standard by hitting 54 homers in 1920, after hitting a then unheard-of 29 in 1919. He captivated the United States and restored interest in our National Pastime with his new style of play. Long live the King!

Likewise, other huge changes have occurred when Mickey retired, and Free Agency restored the balance of power. Baseball needed offense so badly when Mickey retired in 1969 that they lowered the mound from 15 inches to 10 inches.

This was an enormous advantage for the hitters who no longer had to contend with overwhelming down-hill curve balls. So little sliders were newly founded.

It is amazing, and sad, how much this wonderful game has changed so much due to economic forces. Major League Baseball was forced to keep up with operating expenses and nonsensical salaries. Alex "A-Rod" Rodriguez set the bar at one time for 10 years at $252 million. He won one World Series with the Yankees in 2009, surrounded by a great team. Max Scherzer, a future Hall of Famer, gets $30 million a year.

David Price signed for seven years for $217 million, Joe Mauer for eight years for $184 million. Jason Heyward and Miguel Cabrera contracted enormously for 13 years. Giancarlo Stanton signed for an enormous $325 million dollars, handcuffing his Miami and Yankees teams. What a shame.

Free agency shifted the balance of power from the owners' 100-year monopoly to runaway expenses. Since then, baseball authorities were forced to create offense, scoring, and home runs as if everyone was Babe Ruth. Scoring was critical at this juncture with no comparable superstars like Mantle, Mays, and Koufax. That was what our new generation of unsophisticated fans were willing to pay big bucks for. The home run explosion of the new age is meaningless. The mound was lowered, the fences were pulled in, the strike zone was shrunk to a foot or so, and the ball was juiced like never before.

Former manager Sparky Anderson and the great Hall of Famer Stan Musial agreed that, "The new ball is so lively in this era, that at night, it dances all over town." Scott Pitoniak, the award-winning former columnist for the Rochester, New York, *Democrat and Chronicle*, called them "Titlests."

Bill Fischer pitched for many years and gave up Mickey's monumental home run off the Yankee Stadium right-field facade, the longest homer in baseball's history. Fischer had been ripping baseballs open for more than 40 years. I think that most every kid in the 1950s and 1960s did this at one time or another. We would knock the covers off of them and tape them back together with black electrical tape. Once the ball was beyond repair, we would unravel them. It was also a wonderful source of entertainment for a rainy day.

When you opened up a ball back then, as Fischer had also observed, it was like pulling a long string of yarn. In the middle was a pinkish rubber ball that had some bounce.

Today, he claimed, "There is a very resilient nylon-type mesh that surrounds the ball, and on the inside, there are two rubber balls, one surrounds the other. Besides, the seams are so low that the pitchers have a distinct disadvantage throwing a curveball and there is much less surface wind resistance."

Interestingly, after the huge change in 1977, the next big "juice- up" was in 1987. That year, 665 more home runs were hit than there were in 1986, and we haven't stopped this absurdity since. Coincidently, Mark McGwire started his career in 1987. Baseball again ordered an enormous "juice-up" in 1995, purely for the sake of bringing in fans.

Mike North, a veteran sports announcer for a prominent Chicago station, has been a fan and keen observer of baseball his whole life. He revealed the following comments to Paul Susman, which were repeated in a television appearance:

> "When you compare baseballs of the sixties as to now, you notice that the seams on the older baseballs were higher and less tight, where today they are much tighter and sunken. This makes it much tougher for a pitcher to throw a curveball than in the past. I used to watch balls that hit the dirt warning tracks in the sixties, and the ball would bounce maybe two to three feet; now the balls hit the same dirt and regularly bounce eight to 10 feet into the stands. I have seen on the average and smaller players hit the ball on the end of their bats and yet the ball carried into the opposite right-field stands. Ordinary fly balls that used to be caught in the sixties now are carrying into the stands."

A former Major League home run king, who had wished not to be named, said that "Two former Rawlings employees said that 'The modern ball (1977) is wound tighter than Jack Benny was with his dough. This much harder ball can give a hitter an extra 50+ feet on his drives.' In addition, the 1993 ball is tighter than the (former) Chairman of the Fed, Alan Greenspan's control."

Mickey played with a ball that just did not travel all that much. This didn't change until 1977, after he retired. Only Mickey could defy physics and sent to ball to places that were unfathomable. Clark Griffith, the formal owner of the Minnesota Twins, told Susman, "In Mantle's era, pitchers used to put oil on the ball to deaden or freeze them, in a vain attempt to try to stop Mick from hitting it so often out of the park."

The "Baseball Gods" really didn't change the ball until 1977, when the Rawlings Company supplied the major leagues with inferior balls made in Haiti. The number of home runs that were hit in 1977 was increased over 1976 was increased by 32 percent. They should have listened to John J. McGraw, who once said, "When you monkey with ball, you monkey with the game itself."

The pre-1977 "softer" ball and the historic stadiums mandated that only superhuman strength could conquer the enormous distances with any regularity. Mickey hit more astonishing home runs than any man that ever played the cherished game of hardball. He also drove a golf ball colossal distances.

Growing up, I read *SPORT* magazine, and it's fascinating articles often painted very clear images of greatness based on astonishing athletic feats. One article that I distinctly remember addressed the best golfers and their longest drives.

The article stated that the great golfing legends Arnold Palmer and Jack Nicklaus each had 400-yard drives. It was well noted that Mickey had two. I say *at least* two based on the following story told to Paul Susman by his cousin Max Mantle:

> "All the Mantle kids were built like an ox. I knew that I could hit a golf ball a country mile. One day, I took Mickey out to play. We got to a hole where the green was 346 yards away. I boastfully said to Mickey, 'I am going to show you how to hit this damn thing.' I teed off and caught it perfect. It seemed as it would never land and finally landed on the green. I said, 'Let me see you top that drive!' Mickey kinda smirked and lovingly called me a 'little shit.' He coiled back and unleashed a thunderous drive. The ball took off like a rocket ship. It flew past the green, over the next fairway and kept going and going. On the other side of the fairway was an old red barn. The ball cleared the roof of that ol' barn and landed 420 to 430 yards away."

In fact, there were several other 400-foot drives hit at his home course of Preston Trails, in Dallas. For example, Mickey, who was affectionately called "The Commerce Comet," nearly reached a 510-yard hole with a measured 440-yard drive! And if that is not enough: Mickey and Nicklaus were paired in a one-day Pro-Am tournament. Mickey outdrove the great Jack Nicklaus on every hole, including an unbelievable 398-yard 3-wood!

This is not the only course where Mickey hit one of the longest drives in the world. According to the late Arnold Palmer's eye witness, Mickey launched another inconceivable drive.

On the "Monster" course at Firestone, there is a 625-yard hole. Only three men in history had ever reached the green in two shots. "Mickey did it," according to one *SPORT* magazine article, "and only had a SEVEN IRON left!" A very important point to remember here is that the golf balls were not as compressed back then as they are now. Also, with all due respect to Tiger Woods and the new generation of golf superstars, there were no titanium shafts and the other technological improvements of today. There is no question of the differences of both golf balls and baseballs then and now.

Long-time Webster, New York, resident and former Irondequoit High School baseball coach Kenny Slater received a call-up from the Yankees in his playing days. Kenny watched Mickey, in amazement, just a foot and a half away as he was catching batting practice.

"Mickey hit a baseball just like he hit a golf ball," Kenny said. "You would see the impact and hear the crack and *whoosh*; the baseball would travel as if it were shot out of a cannon. He would pummel the upper deck so hard that the ball would bounce all the way back to the infield. Mickey would routinely smash two to three titanic line drives off the face of the roof in batting practice, and the other players would just shake their heads in disbelief, as no one else even hit the facade once."

Kenny went on to say, "When Mickey was hitting in batting practice, every player from both teams stopped whatever they were doing and watched. The stadium would be completely quiet except hearing the tremendous impact.

Not until Mickey was finished would they go back to their business."

Stadiums were a huge factor in hitting homers. Some fences were short, and the wind was a large consideration, too. Hall of Famer Ferguson "Fergie" Jenkins called Wrigley Field "The Sandbox." Atlanta's Fulton County Stadium and Camden Yards were and are "a piece of cake" to get a big fly out of. Atlanta's Chief "Knock-A-Homa" would be exhausted after a doubleheader with Hank Aaron, Joe Adcock, and Eddie Mathews. Likewise, modern parks in Arizona, Florida, and Colorado have air so light and thin that even the smallest size hitters can hit homers off their fists.

Yankee Stadium, Washington's old Griffith Stadium, and Cleveland's Memorial Stadium were massive. Baltimore's Memorial Stadium used to have 445-foot power alleys in Mickey's day.

On August 14, 1955, Eddie Lopat was on the mound. The legendary Paul Richards was in the stands. Richards told Susman, "I saw Mick hit one way farther than that 457-foot shot that Frank Robinson hit down the line. This one landed at the top of the left-center field bleachers and was the longest ball ever hit in Baltimore, over 525 feet."

Mickey stands as the only human being to hit a ball over the left-center-field bleachers at Griffith stadium, he accomplished this several times. The mighty slugger and Hall of Famer Harmon Killebrew, who played there for a while, never did it. Killebrew recalled his reaction at his first glimpse of enormous Griffith Stadium:

> "I'll never forget the day I walked into Griffith Stadium. Like any young hitter, the first thing I looked at was the fences.

To my utter dismay, the left-field fence was over 400 feet away -- and it was 10 feet high to boot! After seeing the dimensions of the whole park, he joked throughout his career, if I had known about the fences in Griffith, I probably would have signed with the Boston Red Sox."

Mickey became the first player in baseball history to hit two home runs in a single game over the centerfield fence in Griffith Stadium, according to the *Democrat and Chronicle*. The first home run bounced off a roof across the street from the stadium. Both homers, which soared for about 500 feet, happened on Opening Day, April 17, 1956. President Eisenhower was there, the April 18 report said, to see the Yankees trounce the Senators, 10 – 4. One of Mick's most astounding blasts occurred in Killebrew's next home park of Minnesota, on May 4, 1961.

Against a mammoth 50-mile-an-hour wind, Mickey hit the scoreboard that was 475 to 480 feet away. The wind was so ferocious that Tony Kubek played the game under protest. He felt that it was unsafe, and the pitcher was actually blown off the mound by the wind's force. This smashed ball, if unimpeded, would have traveled 600 feet.

Incidentally, in a 1961 home run contest at Griffith Stadium, Mickey again blasted the ball over the same bleachers against the wind. Mickey also hit his famous prodigious shot off Chuck Stobbs in this park, which caromed off the football scoreboard. The blast was measured by Red Patterson a mere

565 feet away, although some have recently questioned that it was actually measured. In true flight, the ball would have easily carried 650 feet. In Mickey's career, he pounded at least five mighty shots into the center-field bleachers and one over the flagpole, during regulation play, including two on opening day of 1956, his Triple Crown Year! Very few of the greatest sluggers ever have even hit one 500-foot homer. Mickey also hit two balls that were 31 feet high and passed over the 438-foot marker. One of them hit a tree across the street on the fly. Casey just shook his head in amazement.

In 1953 in Shibe Park, Mickey hit an enormous pinch-hit grand slam that cleared the left-center-field roof at 530 feet. According to the *Chicago Daily News*, quoting the AP wire, Mickey hit the ball "beyond the sight, grasp, or measurement of anyone in the park." It went beyond anyone's imagination, too, including that of Rod Serling.

That same year, Mickey performed the rare feat of clearing the scoreboard above the left-field bleachers in Sportsman Park in St. Louis. That one traveled about 530 feet. In 1951, in Chicago's Comiskey Park, Mickey reached the lower-right corner of center field, 450 feet away, in one second. That shot was undoubtedly one of the hardest balls ever hit in the history of this beloved sport.

At Kansas City Municipal Stadium, in June of 1961, Mickey hit two exceptional homers in one night. One traveled nearly 500 feet and the other went 530 feet. Veteran sports announcer Joe McGruff of Kansas City was absolutely sure that the first shot would have flown 550 feet through the air if the scoreboard had not impeded it.

In the former Cleveland Stadium, Mickey was one of only two players to ever reach the distant center-field bleachers before the fence was brought in, cutting through the winds of

Lake Erie. Mantle's 485- foot shot was considered to be the longer of the two. Slugger Luke Easter hit the other ball, along with another 575-foot shot at the Polo Grounds.

Luke also hit a truly phenomenal blast at the former Silver Stadium for the International League Rochester Red Wings. The ball rocketed over the right-field light tower. Luke was a marvelous slugger, but he never hit more than 31 homers in a season. Likewise, Moose Skowron, who went to Purdue on a football scholarship and then opted for baseball, was one of a very few that reached the Yankee bleachers. Moose never hit more than 28 homers.

New York Yankee Elston Howard, 1963 American League MVP and fifth in slugging that campaign, also had extraordinary strength and agility and hit some of the longest homers at Yankee Stadium. He, too, never surpassed 28 homers. But 28 home runs were very admirable because that was the era when conditions were real.

Howard was so strong that even in his later years he could put on a display of awesome strength, as told to me by a local publisher:

> "Elston was a coach in his later years. After their great win over the Dodgers in the 1977 World Series, the main Series star was having a 'hoot and holler.' Strutting around and being the BMOC, he pushed Ellie, who was always a humble and dignified human being. Ellie told him to lay-off. As one might expect, the star came back with another and bit harder shove. Ellie merely warned him a little firmer tone. When the third shove came, Ellie picked him up by the seat of his

pants and his shirt and walked him over to the clubhouse garbage can and deposited him, head first!"

When Mickey was 19 years old, he was sent down from the Yankees to the K.C. Blues for a short time. Mickey had a fantastic night at Swayne Field in Toledo. He only drove in three runs, but he did go five-for-five with two home runs, a triple, a double, and single. His last home run, however, was unforgettable. According to Susman, the ball left the yard at a height of 200 feet and the 370-foot mark and then flew over a distant gas station.

Most sluggers hit well at friendly Tiger Stadium. Frank Howard and Harmon Killebrew each cleared the left-field roof one time. Reggie Jackson hit the transformer on the roof as a pinch hitter in the 1971 All-Star game, when there was a gale wind of 45 miles per hour blowing out. Ted Williams cleared the right-field roof once. Mickey, batting both righty and lefty, hit the roof at least four times and cleared the roof three times. Three of those shots were into stiff winds! One cleared the light tower!!

One of these ferocious blasts was off Art Houterman in Detroit on June 11, 1953. It left the field at the 370-foot mark over 145 feet high and was still on the rise. The ball skyrocketed off the right-center field roof. The Detroit paper said that it would have landed two streets away on the fly.

"That ball was hit so hard that I thought that the whole stadium was going to collapse," Casey Stengel recalled. Joe Ginsberg, the Detroit catcher, vividly recalled this mammoth shot, saying, "The ball was hit with such force that it stayed up in the lights for what seemed to be like a half an hour." Umpire Larry Knapp said that "Mantle's shot hit the top of the tower with no wind and Reggie's 1971 All Star blast hit the base with a gale wind behind him."

In 1958, pitching for Detroit at home, was the great Jim Bunning. Mickey was an easy-going guy unless you pissed him off. Bunning was foolish enough to brushback Mantle. Mickey proceeded to let loose and hit the ball over the roof of Briggs Stadium. The ball continued across Trumbull Avenue at about 30 feet high and hit a cab company. The AP wire stated that there was a stiff wind blowing in. As Casey would say, "If you don't believe me, you can look it up."

What is not well known is that Mickey, on at least seven occasions hit balls that had more than ample velocity and torque to leave Yankee Stadium. Foxx, Howard, and Killebrew reached the distant left-field upper stands once apiece. Mickey did it four times.

Two of these blasts were hit fiercely enough to leave the park without the wind being a factor. On September 13, 1953, Mickey unloaded against Billy Hoeft. The ball was hit into the left-center-field seats near the bullpen with such force that it rebounded all the way back to the playing field. It soared over the 425 feet and 80 feet above the ground and was clearly still rising upon impact. McDougald said, "That ball was hit much harder than the one he hit off of Stobbs." Bill Dickey stated, "This revolutionary shot topped the famous Jimmy Foxx 550-foot homer off Lefty Grove in 1936."

On August 23, 1956, Mickey hit another astounding shot off Chicago's Paul LaPalme. Les Moss, the former American League catcher and manager, said that it was the longest ball that he ever saw over his career. LaPalme said, "It was hit so hard and so fast that no one knew where it was. Suddenly, there was a loud blast some 550-600 feet away that was so loud upon impact that it sounded like an explosion." Mickey also hit a 457-foot triple that day.

None of the left-handed sluggers, including Ruth and Jackson, ever hit one off the right-field facade. Mickey accomplished this incredible feat five times. Against Ray Burtschy on May 6, 1956, Mickey slammed the ball so violently against the upper facade, near the line, that the ball rebounded 100 feet to the right-field bullpen.

On May 30, 1956, Mickey connected off Pedro Ramos, who hit Mantle on his previous meeting during the previous contest. The ball missed going out of old Yankee Stadium by 18 inches. Frank Crosetti, a contemporary of Ruth, Gehrig, and Foxx, said, "I saw Foxx hit his tremendous homer off Gomez. It was the longest I ever saw until this one." Bill Dickey, the great Yankee catcher from that golden era, commented after seeing this gargantuan blast, "Mantle hits a ball harder than Ruth, Foxx, or Gehrig. And take it from me, also farther than any man I have seen."

The Guinness Book of World Records lists the longest home run ever hit as Mickey's stupendous 643-foot shot at the Detroit Tigers' Briggs Stadium on September 10, 1960. That is where it hit on the fly.

Mickey hit another amazing left-handed homer at the University of Southern California against the Trojans on March 26, 1951. The Yankees played USC as their last warm-up game before traveling back to New York. The USC center fielder watched the ball leave the park over the right-field fence, where it continued to sail over an adjacent football field and short-hopped off the fence that surrounded the entire sports complex. The distance was measured at 660 feet away. Astonishingly, later that same game, Mickey unloaded a miraculous right-handed drive that was nearly as long as the first. The ball landed on the porch of a house beyond the left-field fence.

Rod Dedeaux, the famous long-time USC coach and eyewitness to both hits, said, "The second was almost as long as the first." He also testified that, "These two shots were the longest in history." That day, Mickey drove in seven runs with two homers, a bases-loaded triple and a single.

Babe Ruth's longest home runs were hit in Tampa, in a spring training game, when he was playing for the Boston Red Sox. It measured nearly 600 feet. Mickey's exhibition shots at USC far surpassed Ruth's. Mickey's homers went further than Ruth's in St. Louis, Detroit, Pittsburgh, Boston, Chicago, and New York.

By some reports, the great Josh Gibson of the Monarch Grays of the Negro League hit one out of Yankee Stadium. That was never substantiated. As a matter of fact, Josh refuted that statement himself. In speaking with the late Clete Boyer in Cooperstown one afternoon, he told me, "Mickey and Pepitone were having a contest in batting practice one day to see if either of them could hit the ball clear out of Yankee Stadium! Mickey was the toughest when you got him mad and Pepitone egged him on." Pepitone was extremely strong and lanky in his own right and could slam a tremendous poke himself. Mickey wouldn't have any of the ribbing and losing to Pepitone. Boyer said that, "Mickey hit a breathtaking shot, and it went out of the stadium, but recalled that particular blast as being foul."

Boyer concluded, "I have never seen anything like that shot." Mickey was like Babe Ruth in "getting up for the big one." He was an easy-going guy but watch out if you got him riled up. When Pedro Ramos hit Mickey and Jim Bunning threw that brushback pitch, they paid the price.

According to sportswriter Maury Allen, Mickey hit a fair ball out of Yankee Stadium in batting practice. Allen was an eyewitness to this and testified without even the slightest quiver in his statement that Mickey indisputably did the impossible. He told Susman that the ball left Yankee Stadium at 200 feet high and it disappeared. Eyewitnesses said that it went over the tracks of the L-Train on the fly.

Mickey's close friend Lewis Early testified that Mickey, who was extremely shy about his prodigious drives, confided in him that he did hit a fair ball out of Yankee Stadium in batting practice.

Mickey himself acknowledged that his second moonshot off the Yankee Stadium facade, against Bill Fischer on May 23, 1963, was the longest, hardest ball that he ever hit. Former Kansas City coach Jimmy Dykes, who vividly remembered the longest blasts of Gehrig, Ruth, Foxx, and Greenberg, commented, "That was the hardest ball that any man had ever hit. Also, the wind was no factor as there was a slight wind blowing against him that night."

Hearing this mammoth shot live on radio that May evening, I will never forget the announcer saying, "Mantle swings and that ball is gone and *still rising*! Oh my God, I think it is out of the Stadium!" And then a tremendously loud, ringing *thud* came over the air. Kubek had likened it to a cannon exploding at Gettysburg. With the impact, the ball caromed back almost to the infield.

The ball hit within inches of the top of the facade, which was on top of the roof back then. It was still on the rise, and if the stadium was back about six to 10 feet, the ball would have cleared the stadium. The ball struck the stadium 656 feet away still rising. Two independent qualified experts knew all the essential elements: the distance, the angle, and the impact based on reverberation almost back to the infield. They also knew the time of flight based on the radio replay. The ball traveled at least 230 feet per second. One estimated that the ball would have traveled 732 feet; the other calculated the distance at 734 feet. Take your pick.

Mickey Mantle has the documented longest home runs ever hit: seven or more at old Yankee Stadium, five at Washington's Griffith Stadium, four at Briggs Stadium, three at Cleveland Memorial, two each at Fenway Park and Baltimore Memorial, and one each at Comiskey Park, Kansas City Municipal Stadium, Forbes Field in Pittsburgh, and St. Louis's Sportsman Park. Growing up in the '50s and '60s was great because hitting 50 homers in a season was the supreme benchmark for all of baseball history. If you could not name the players who accomplished this, you were not a real baseball fan. Babe Ruth had done so for four seasons. Mickey, Mays, Foxx, and Kiner achieved this feat twice each. Greenberg, "Hack" Wilson, Maris, and Mize had all done it once.

You also had to know who Carl Hubbell struck out in the 1934 All-Star game: Ruth, Gehrig, Foxx, Simmons, and Cronin. Furthermore, you were most likely to know the starting lineup of all 16 teams and at least their first three pitchers.

Hitting 40 homers pre-1977 is just like hitting 55 or more homers now. If McGwire had 70, then Mickey would have between 95 and 110, just by the fence differences, even with the old ball.

During Mickey's 18 years in the league, from 1951 to 1968, the home run champions of the American League averaged 42 home runs per season; in the National League, champs averaged just under 45. The group of home run leaders for each year, listed in *Total Baseball*, averaged 33 in the American

League and 41 in the National League. In the same era, the champion hit in the 30 range. Only three men reached the 50-plus plateau: Mantle, Maris, and Mays.

The most amazing feat is to win the Triple Crown, awarded to the player with the highest batting average, most home runs, and most runs batted in (RBIs). This remarkable feat has only been accomplished 17 times by truly great players. Only Mickey has won the Triple Crown with more than 50 homers (353, 52, 130) in 1956.

McGwire had tremendous strength not unlike Killebrew, who had a career high of 49 home runs. Frank Howard and Dave Kingman never hit 50 homers in a season. Hank Aaron, who hit 755 homers over his career, and Mike Schmidt, with eight home run titles, never did, either. The same goes for other great sluggers, like Gehrig, DiMaggio, Eddie Mathews, Ernie Banks, Luke Easter, Ted Kluszewski, the great Ted Williams, Frank Robinson, Rocky Colavito, Mel Ott, Duke Snider, Willie McCovey, Willie Stargell, Reggie Jackson, Albert Pujols, Frank Thomas, and Eddie Murray. A-Rod had one 50-home run year, which was questionable; so, did David Ortiz.

If he had played before 1977, McGwire would have been in the true slugger range of 40 to 49 homers in his prime. Jim Thome would have been, too. Ken Griffey, Jr., who was an exceptional ball player, might have hit 30 to 40, as would have Barry Bonds. Rafael Palmeiro had only natural warning track power. None of these players by any stretch of the imagination could come close to an authentic slugger like Luke Easter.

Ken Griffey, Jr., complained of his new ballpark, Safeco Field, where the fences were 10 feet further and the air was heavy. From *Sports Illustrated*: "The balls flew out of the Kingdom but after moving to the new field, things changed.

Griffey knows it might cost him the home run record. Balls hit in the air died."

One night after yet another one of his well-struck fly balls had died in an opposing outfielder's glove, Griffey called Woody Woodward, the Seattle General Manager at the time, from the dugout phone. "Get me out of this place. Trade me right now!"

Maybe Griffey would like to try "Death Valley" of old Yankee Stadium, with the old ball and an expanded strike zone!

During Sammy Sosa's June 1998 barrage of home runs, the press marveled at one that cleared Wrigley's wall and hit the first house on the street about 450 feet away. In 1999, Sosa hit a second one that traveled about 480 feet. According to Susman, Mickey once hit a ball out of Sportsman Park and hit the sixth house up on Second Street, on the fly, 636 feet away. As Mel Allen used to muse, "How about that?"

Now we have the "Age of Entertainment," which is clearly a "show for dough." So, let's see, we have a *very* juiced-up ball with much flatter seams, pitching hills instead of mounds, a strike zone that is the size of the side of a shoebox, and fences that have been moved in drastically. Pitchers throw to pumped-up weightlifters, who are likely taking muscle-enhancing drugs and possibly illegal PEDs, too. The power alleys may be 100 feet shorter and into significantly thinner air. The bats are so enhanced that you can break them over your knee.

Just imagine if Mickey had grown up in the 1980s and '90s. He would have gone to college on a baseball scholarship. Warm weather schools like USC or Arizona State would be less conducive to pulled muscles and better for stretching out. Or better yet, how about the University of Colorado, near

Coors Field, at 5,280 feet above sea level, where the ball just keeps traveling and traveling? Mickey would have lifted and conditioned like he never needed to do. Someone would have egged Mickey on about being a wimp at only 5'11" tall and 175 pounds at that time of his life. Mickey would proceed to uncoil one his thunderous swings. After a massive CRACK and a WOOSH, one could only sense the direction of the ball. The human eye couldn't actually see where the ball landed. Satellites would have to then project the images of the landing. Mickey's homers would no longer be measured by feet or meters. The next morning's paper would read: **"Mantle's Homer Orbits One-fifth of a Mile."**

2

HITTING THE BALL SQUARELY

"I wanted to be the greatest hitter who ever lived."
– Ted Williams

From the time you start in Little League, your coach implores you to "hit the ball squarely": a round sphere meeting a round bat. It is so difficult that we make national heroes out of people who fail seven out of 10 times. Some say that "hitting the ball squarely" is the hardest thing to do in sports. Others disagree with this assessment.

The arguments have been played out often. The ball is round; the bat is round. The pitcher has a curve, splitter, knuckler, two-humped blooper, and where "the bottom falls out," not to mention a tenacious will to win. The coach screams, "Hit the ball squarely, on a line and exactly in the gap, behind the runner!"

If you're a baseball player, you can easily understand the difficulty of hitting and easily fight your side of the argument. Ted Williams was arguably the best "pure hitter" who ever lived. He had a ferocious might and ferocious forearms, too.

He used to do at least fifty fingertip pushups a day to keep his physical edge. He often had some great "Top Dog" battles with Mantle during a game. Mickey would hit one 15 rows up in the bleachers, and Ted would top him by seven rows. Mickey would get up later in the game and blast another one, 30 rows up. Ted would follow with another prodigious blast, landing yet a few rows further! Mickey quite often would win their next personal contest.

After retiring with 521 home runs, Ted managed the Washington Senators for a spell. He was also friends with two-time Olympic gold medal decathlon champion Bob Mathias.

They argued for what seemed like eons, with Ted proclaiming that the hardest thing to do in any sport was hit a home run. Bob countered that nearly everyone who had played baseball had hit a home run. "The hardest thing to do in a sport," Bob had said, "is to hold an individual world record for any single event." The friendly debate went on with each meeting.

Mathias became a U.S. Congressman in Washington. During one fundraiser, he played in a hardball game (Democrats vs. Republicans) at Washington's Griffith Stadium. Coincidentally, Ted Williams was near first base when Mathias stepped into the batter's box. Although Morris Udall, the U.S. Democratic Congressman from Arizona, pitched only a lob, which is actually harder to hit deep, the great Olympic champion promptly parked it over the center-field fence! As he started to circle the bases, he wasn't sure what the scowl on Ted's face meant. Breaking into a smile, Ted then cordially took off his cap and tipped it.

Ted made an art out of studying opposing pitchers beyond the physical aspects of hitting the ball. The few times that Ted didn't rip the ball, he would think and plan his next attack.

If a pitcher made him look bad or got him out in a crucial situation, he would always remember the pitch location, count, spin, and speed. If not the next meeting, eventually he would get even. Once, he had to go even further to "get his man."

Ray Scarborough was a good pitcher when he was with the Washington Senators. His record was about .500 for some pretty bad teams. As age was catching up to him, he was hanging onto his big-league career in the late 1940s. His claim to fame was that "he had Ted Williams's number." Ted couldn't hit a loud foul off him, which was truly amazing. It was also downright embarrassing.

Williams, in fact, was the one who asked Red Sox owner Tom Yawkey to buy Scarborough from the Chicago White Sox. Once Scarborough was signed to the Red Sox, Yawkey ordered him to pitch batting practice to Williams.

At first, Williams couldn't touch him. After a few weeks of seeing the pitch selection, Williams had a few good pokes. This routine lasted over the 1951 and part of the 1952 seasons. As time went on, everything that Scarborough served up, Williams hit it squarely. Ted now had *his* number.

Soon thereafter, Ted walked into Yawkey's office and said, "I've got him, so now you can get rid of him." Immediately, Yawkey put him up on waivers, and the Yankees picked him up for $10,000. With the Yankees, Scarborough beat the Red Sox. Sweet revenge!

Ted also saw another kid "hit the ball squarely" one night. In the spring of 1956 at Yankee Stadium, Williams saw Mantle hit what he said was "the hardest ball I've ever seen hit off a Red Sox pitcher." Right-hander George Susce threw a fastball, and Mantle hit a rising line drive to right. It smashed into a seat high up in the third deck still carrying some 415 feet from home plate.

Tom Brewer, another Red Sox pitcher, said, "If the seat hadn't stopped that one, the ball woulda gone out of the Stadium and maybe out of the Bronx."

After Mantle hit the facade the first time, off Pedro Ramos, Williams commented, "He's a once-in-a-lifetime ballplayer." Ted was, indeed, the ultimate authority on hitting the ball squarely.

3

YOU'RE ON THE "SPIT LIST"

"Cheating is baseball's oldest profession. No other game is so rich in skullduggery, so suited to it or so proud of it."
– Thomas Boswell

In 1920, baseball had to clean up its act. Thank God for Babe Ruth. The presidents of each league had begun to firmly rule on the baseballs used and the rules of pitching, including that of "freak delivers." It wasn't until November of 1920 that a real Commissioner was put into office. History *does* repeat itself.

In 1920, pitching rules defined "ball defacing" as any intentional tampering with the ball, such as rubbing it with soil or applying foreign substances like rosin, paraffin, or licorice to it. The rules also prohibited intentionally damaging or "roughening" the ball with sandpaper, emery paper, or other tools. Pitchers were not allowed to "expectorate" on the ball or glove; nor could they deliver what was known as a "shine" ball, "mud" ball, "emery" ball, or "spitball." Players caught using defaced baseballs would be barred from the game.

If you didn't know how to cheat at baseball before, you certainly have a nice menu of options now.

Gaylord Perry, Hall of Famer, allegedly would have spent the remainder of his life in jail for all the greasers he loaded up. Now you can spit on the umpire and continue to play in the League Championship Series. Where are we going? In the old days, the great managers and dedicated owners would have sat the kid down immediately. Peter Angelos should have been ashamed of himself.

At the time of this ruling, 17 primary spitball pitchers from both leagues received an exemption from the rule until the ends of their careers. In the American League, exempt players included A.W. Ayers, Ray Caldwell, Stanley Coveleskie, Urban Faber, H.B. Leonard, Jack Quinn, Allan Russell, Urban Shocker, and Allan Sothoron. For the National League, the list included William Doak, Phil Douglas, Dana Fillingim, Ray Fisher, Marvin Goodwin, Clarence Mitchell, Richard Rudolph, and Burleigh Grimes.

Grimes, who won 270 games and was inducted into the Hall of Fame, was undoubtedly the best complete pitcher on the list. He didn't rely solely on his "spitter" and was a tough-nosed competitor. He played the longest and was traded to Brooklyn, in a multi-player trade with Pittsburgh for Casey Stengel. He then played for Wilbert "Uncle Robbie" Robinson. Later, he was traded to the Giants and played for the infamous John J. McGraw.

In examining this list, I don't see Don Newcombe of "Dem Bums," Lew Burdette of Milwaukee, Don Sutton, Joe Niekro, Mike Scott, or Gaylord Perry. The latter threw a "shine" ball with so much Vaseline smeared on it that it would catch the glare of the sun on its flight to the plate. Only Perry and Niekro, however, actually got caught defacing the ball.

4

A "REAL" NO-HITTER

My wife Jill was a fabulous elementary school teacher. She often spelled words phonetically and discussed literal translations with her students.

We have had many discussions about no-hitters and perfect games. She often asks, "How can this be a no-hitter when there was a fly out, ground out, or even a foul ball hit?" The older I get, the more I listen to her.

Has any individual in the history of this great game ever pitch a real no-hitter? Undoubtedly, the answer is just three human beings. The first and only hardball pitcher who could do this *very improbable* task was the unparalleled Leroy "Satchel" Paige. He was absolutely the best pitcher who ever played the game. He was far better than Denton True "Cy" Young, Nolan Ryan, Walter "Big Train" Johnson, Christy "Big Six" Mathewson, and Sandy Koufax.

Nolan Ryan had only seven pseudo no-hitters. Together, these five magnificent fire-ballers won an outstanding total of 2,056 games with a winning percentage of .644. The best winning percentage of all time is .690, held by Whitey Ford, of the great Yankee dynasty. Ron Guidry holds the "official" best winning percentage for one season (1978) of .893, with an astounding record of 25 – 3, but mistakenly wasn't named the MVP of the American League!

"Robert Leroy Satchel (sometimes Satchell) Paige pitched at least 2,500 games in his professional career," Richard Donovan wrote in "The Fabulous Satchel Paige." "He won an incomprehensible total of over 2,000 games while traveling 30,000 miles per year, at times, for a winning percentage of .769! Satch shut out the opponents at least 250 times and spun at least 45 pseudo no-hitters!" The question is, were any of those *real* no hitters? The answer is that some probably were, as we will see. National advertisements boasted, "Satchel Paige, World's Greatest Pitcher, and Guaranteed to Strike out the First Nine Men." Most often, he would. As he proceeded to make good on his promise, Donovan said, "Satchel, who pitched for the Monarch Grays and various other Negro League teams, would call in the outfielders and have them sit on the edge of the outfield grass. His infielders would watch from a squatting position. The few times that he did not accomplish this feat, the crowd would be so disappointed that sometimes he had to flee for his life." So often did he mow down the first nine with nary a swing or any contact whatsoever. What's the big deal about doing this three times in succession?

Roger Clemens has two 20-strikeout games. Max Scherzer and Kerry Woods had also "K'ed" 20. Steve Carlton, Tom "Terrific" Seaver, and David Cone each had one 19-strikeout game apiece, and Randy Johnson had two. Koufax, Guidry and Bob Feller all fanned 18. Tom Cheney of the Washington Senators once struck out 21 batters in a 16-inning game. Bob Gibson struck out 17 Tigers during the 1968 World Series.

According to Donovan, "Paige averaged an implausible 15 strikeouts per game, five days a week! Satchel Paige stuck out the great Rogers Hornsby five times in one game and 22 batters in an exhibition game against major leaguers. Satchel possessed super human powers and could do things that no other man alive could." Donovan also offers up this anecdote:

> "Satch walked into the shower and his teammates were desperately trying to toss a slippery, wet cake of soap into a wall dish and have it stick. Nobody had ever been successful at this artful pastime. Satchel tried it and incredibly 'stuck it' the first two times and remarked, 'Boys, there is apparently things that even I don't know that I can do.'"

George Will's fabulous *Men at Work* tells of the great Satchel in two remarkable and factual vignettes:

> "Whitey Herzog was playing for the Miami Marlins of the International League. The Marlins once had a distance-throwing contest before a night game. Herzog clearly recalled, '(Don) Landrum and I had the best arms of any outfielders. We were out by the center-field fence, throwing two-hoppers to the plate. Ol' Satch came out, didn't even warm up, and kind of flipped the ball sidearm. It went 400 feet on a dead line and hit the plate. I wouldn't believe it if I hadn't seen it.'"

As Herzog himself explained, "'We were on the road one night in Rochester, N.Y., screwing around in the outfield. They had a hole in the outfield fence just barely big enough for a baseball to go through, and the deal was that any player that hit a ball through there on the fly, would win $10,000!'"

I (your author) grew up in Rochester and watched hundreds of games at old beautiful Red Wing Stadium, later named Silver Stadium. The hole-in- the-wall contest was downright *impossible*.

"I tried to throw the ball through the hole 150 – 200 times and didn't even come close, so I went back to the dugout," Herzog said. He continued:

> "When Satch got to the park (naturally at his own pace and schedule, not to jangle his stomach juices) I said, 'Satch, I bet you can't throw the ball through the hole out there.'
>
> "He looked and said, 'Wild Child, does the ball fit in the hole?'
>
> "'Yeah Satch,' I said, 'But not by much. I'll bet you a fifth of Old Forester that you can't throw it through there.' "'Wild Child,' he said, 'I'll see you tomorrow night.'"

The next night, Satchel showed up early for batting practice. Herzog went to the outfield and stepped about six and a half feet away from the hole in the wall. "Satch ambled out there, took the ball, brought it up to his eye like he was aiming and let fire," Herzog said. "I couldn't believe it. The ball hit the hole, rattled around, and dropped back out. Satch took another ball and drilled the hole dead center. The ball went right through the hole! Nobody ever before or after has ever accomplished that trick. 'Thank you Wild Child,' Satch said, and then strolled back to the clubhouse."

A few years later in 1958, Satch returned to Red Wing Stadium and again pitched for the Miami Marlins. He took his usual stroll out to the mound and easily polished off the young Rochester Red Wings.

I couldn't tell you how old he was that day, but he admitted to being in his *late* fifties. I'm not sure if even Satch knew his exact age for sure. According to Donovan, Satchel's grandfather kept his birth certificate in a Bible. One day, his grandfather left the Bible outside, where the family goat got a hold of it and ate it.

The great Satch had more pitches than Carter's had little liver pills. Many pitchers had great success with fewer pitches. Christy Mathewson had his fadeaway, Nolan Ryan had the express, Hoyt Wilhelm had the butterfly, and Juan Marichal had a million different angles and speeds. Amos Rusie, the superstar of the 1890s, had his "hummer"; Eddie Cicotte, the ace of the 1919 "Black Sox," had his "shine ball." Mordecai Brown, who holds the second-lowest ERA for starting pitchers ever, had his peculiar spin due to severely injured fingers. Brooklyn's Don Newcombe had a great "spitter," and "Catfish" Hunter owned the "black of the plate" with his slider. All were darn good, but none had the magnificent repertoire of Satchel and were as effective.

Along with Satchel's mystique, his impeccable control and "Long Tom" fastball are clearly the reasons for his overriding greatness. Satchel's fastball had a hop at the end like Walter Johnson's, Bob Feller's and Lefty Grove's, but after the hop, *his* seemed to disappear.

Growing up, we often heard the story of Satchel's disappearing ball. As lore has it, Josh Gibson, the great Monarch catcher, would tell Satch to just to wind up in the dusk and pitch without ever actually delivering the ball. Josh would move to frame the ball and pound his mitt, as to catch it with two hands. The umpire would respond by calling strike after strike on the location where Gibson would *catch* "Long Tom." Then, Josh would *fire* the ball back to Satch, and he would pound his glove. Now, how could that not be a real no-hitter?

All savvy baseball authorities realize that a pitcher's speed is the least important component for success. The first two important factors are movement and location. The gifted Catfish Hunter had a ball that rarely flattened out and superb control of "the black" of the plate. His fastball was not the caliber of Bob Gibson's nor Nolan Ryan's. But Catfish is certainly a praiseworthy Hall of Famer.

Satchel's best asset was his faultless control. During one tryout, Donovan says, Satchel placed a small matchbox on an upright stick next to home plate. He managed to knock it off the stick 13 out of 20 pitches from the mound. At another tryout in his late forties, Manager and Hall of Fame shortstop Lou Boudreau doubted that Satchel could still pitch with that same sense of control. He threw 46 strikes out of 50 pitches and ultimately proved Boudreau wrong.

As Donovan explains, "The bigger the major-league stars, the more Paige bore down. According to accounts passed down by witnesses, he struck out Rogers Hornsby five times in one game, Charlie Gehringer three times in another, Jimmy Foxx three times in a third."

Perhaps the best story of Satchel's sense of control comes from the man himself, as quoted by Donovan: "We were playin' St. Louis for the second half title and leadin' by three games. Bill Gatewood, he lives in Moberly, Missouri, now, was managin' our club. 'Satch,' he said, 'I want you to pitch close to the handle of these boys. Dust them off.' Satch did exactly as told, busting the first three batters' thumbs."

Satchel's exploits provided the ultimate intimidation. The opposing manager quickly threatened to pull his team off the field if Satchel continued to pitch. Refusing to leave, Satchel and his teammates earned yet another championship. They say that pitching is 90 percent of the game. Sorry, Yogi -- this time, it *was* over before it was over!

In 1948, Satchel was named the Rookie of the Year in the American League, probably 25 or 30 years past his prime. Satchel was simply a legend in his own time. One of his students was Mamie "Peanut" Johnson born in 1935. She was the first female pitcher to play in the Negro League. According to the book *A Strong Right Arm* by Michelle Y. Green, Johnson stood 5 feet, 3 inches had a deceptive fastball, slider, change, curveball and screwball. Her record was 33-8 and hit .270 for her career!

Eddie "The King" Feigner was born when Satchel was a young man in the Negro Leagues. His softball pitching record equals that of Paige's hardball lifetime record. Feigner struck out 135,000 batters in winning 8,500 of 10,000 games pitched. He also used only four fielders (including himself and three others) against a full team for his opponents. The "King and His Court" have ruled since 1945, up until a few years ago.

Feigner could deliver his 100- to 110-mile-per-hour risers for strikes from beyond second base on a hardball diamond while blindfolded! He had 930 pseudo no-hitters, and some undoubtedly were real.

Feigner once won 187 consecutive games. He also

astonished a national television audience by baffling Willie Mays, Willie McCovey, Brooks Robinson, Maury Wills, Harmon Killebrew, and Roberto Clemente, as they all struck out in succession.

Like Paige, Feigner traveled the country, logging nearly 60,000 miles per year. During his career, he entertained nearly 20 million fans. Paige and Feigner both had strikeouts in great quantities, tremendous movement of their pitches, and pinpoint control.

At least one pro softball player has achieved the feat of a true no- hitter: Jennie Finch, a collegiate All-American and Olympic medal- winning softball pitcher. *Time* magazine has described her as the most famous softball player in history.

Jennie had two scoreless 35-inning streaks as a pitcher for the Arizona Wildcats. She also had a 40-game win streak and pitched eight no-hitters. In the professional circuit, she pitched her first no- hitter for the Chicago Bandits, striking out 17; most did not even hit a foul ball. In the Pepsi All-Star Game in 2004, Finch struck out future Hall of Famer Albert Pujols, Hall of Famer Mike Piazza, and Brian Giles. Giles said, "I didn't come close to making any contact!"

Paige, Feigner, and Finch have most likely pitched "real no-hitters." The only unanswered question is whether any pitch, during these real no-hitters, was called a ball, stopping these phenomenal pitchers from accomplishing the consummate feat of hurling a "real perfect game."

Thank you, Jill, for raising the bar of greatness.

5

TO DH OR NOT TO DH? WHAT A RIDICULOUS QUESTION!

"The DH [designated hitter rule] serves one useful purpose. It relieves the manager of all responsibility except to post the lineup card on the dugout wall and to make sure that everyone gets to the airport on time."
– Bill "Spaceman" Lee, retired pitcher

Actually, Bill "Spaceman" Lee, the one-time Red Sox pitcher, must be commended on this one. His moon and stars must have been lined up congruently. If nothing else, in 1973, his head was more together than John A. Heydler's, the former National League president, who first came up with this crazy idea in 1928.

The designated hitter (DH) rule was formally presented to the MLB Playing Rules Committee by the Pacific Coast League president in 1961. The recommendation lay dormant until the International League adopted it as an experiment in 1969. American League owners adopted the DH as a three-year experiment late in 1972, after eight of 12 league clubs lost money and nine failed to draw one million fans.

With this great experiment, we force pitchers to become specialist, one-dimensional players by designating other players to hit for them. The managers now want five or six innings if that, and only 100 pitches every fifth day, for some phenomenal salary. And you're going to tell me that this is for the *good of the game*?

What an experiment! This is almost as stupid as playing baseball on perfectly smooth green concrete, where players with weak arms can shoot marbles across the infield and be called "brilliant." Are we going against the natural laws of physics and baseball, or what?

The rule should be referred to as the "Designated Unavailing Hitter" experiment: DUH. It has outlived its worth and should have ended after the initial three-year timeline. Harry Caray, the late announcer for the Chicago Cubs, needs to send down the conclusion of this chapter. What a *real* gift from heaven that would be.

How about all the beanball wars that are going on in the American League? Before Roger Clemens was a Yankee, he freely plunked Yankee third baseman Scott Brosius in the middle of the back. Tino Martinez, the Yankees first base slugger, got hit so hard that he wasn't right for six weeks. Jarred Wright, Cleveland's flame-thrower, got pulled into the president's office for head hunting. Clemens also had his beaning of Mike Piazza and the infamous bat incident in the 2000 Subway Series.

But these pitchers, and all other guilty ones, never have to get into the batter's box and be targets of retaliation. The Orioles and the Red Sox had a tremendous feud in 2017, and the league had to step in. At least when the Giants threw at Bryce Harper, the pitchers had to get in the batter's box.

The DH players cannot field or throw and don't really have to run that much, either. Some got ridiculously bulky by taking muscle enhancers and steroids and lifting weights in the recent era. Then they merely swing from their heels, average maybe a whopping .245, and hit 25 moderate fly balls for $20 million or so a year. If they *connect*, they can waddle around the bases.

The managers don't even have a chance to think anymore. (God forbid a catcher calls a game.) They just have a computer whiz kid enter past data into the program, and the whole chess match is determined by the first batter or first move. Sit back, relax, and watch "Robo-Baseball." Wow, what excitement and critical strategy. Let's charge a lot more to support these inept players and artificial games and see if the consumer will pay?

Baby Boomers have the expendable capital for entertainment. They, for the most part, also have an understanding of *real* baseball and not just home run ball. We should demand a better product.

6

THE "FAIR" LINE

One sunny day, I was walking my Westie, Higgins Nolan Ryan Kravetz. We were pulling and tugging across the school hardball diamond and just crossing over from fair to foul territory. Higgy stopped abruptly, lifted his leg, and relieved himself. For the first time in history, the line was truly foul.

Whoever started this "foul line" thing must have been in a drunken stupor after pitching a real no-hitter. But why hasn't the name "foul line" been changed for over 100 years?

Tim McCarver, the long-time major league catcher who turned to broadcasting and analyzing, has addressed this and pleaded his case. McCarver is an excellent analyst because he caught for so long. In our chat, McCarver said, "When the whole game is in front of you, your perspective is different than most."

Better yet, how could we have expected any significant positive changes without a real Commissioner of Baseball? For that matter, could there have been any progress for the good of the game? Finally, we have Rob Manfred. Obviously, the foul line issue is just one small item. But the evolution of the "foul" line and some controversial plays that have surrounded the rulings are interesting.

The Playing Rules for 1857 stated that if a ball first touches the ground, or is caught without having touched the ground, either on or in front of the range of those bases (home and first, and home and third base), it shall be considered fair.

In 1870, a *fair ball* was defined as ball in fair territory, the part of the playing field within and including the first and third baselines, from home base to the bottom of the playing field fence and perpendicularly upwards. All foul lines are in fair territory.

What a revelation! And we still accept calling the playing lines the *foul lines* after all this time? What progress we have made! At least 1954 rules finally enforced that the players had to remove their gloves from the field of play between defensive innings. The Infield Fly Rule is more complicated than the Foul Line rules and has been part of the game since 1895.

The late Willie "Stretch" McCovey, the San Francisco Giants' Hall of Fame slugging first basemen, was instrumental in changing the height of the *fair poles*. He hit moonshots that towered far higher than the old poles. The old rules stated that the poles needed to be at least 10 feet high. The umpires proved themselves as human by blowing some calls with no clear point of reference. They finally acquiesced and agreed that they needed higher poles, but that didn't always guarantee a correct call.

The great Hall of Famer Roberto Clemente was the star of the 1971 World Series, hitting .414 with clutch homers off premier pitchers Jim Palmer and Mike Cuellar of the *New Orioles*. Roberto was an incredible magician with the bat. He could take a pitch that was deep inside on his hands and still hit it to right field. During his career, he would often "fake out" the umpire to where the ball was going because of his uncanny ability to perform in a most unorthodox style. During the 1972 League Championship Series, he had a terrific inside-out swing and hit the ball out of the park in right field, inside the *fair* pole. The home plate umpire was shocked and missed the call, ruling the ball went foul. Clemente was burning. He drove the next pitch into the left-field stands to give the umpire a better look at the *fair* pole.

In 1972, Roberto Clemente was playing in his last postseason, before he tragically died on New Year's Eve in a plane crash, carrying food and medical supplies to earthquake-stricken Nicaragua. Clemente had a lifetime average of .317 and had also just collected his coveted 3,000th hit on his last-ever season plate appearance.

Clemente, with a very classy move, had announced that he would sit out the last few games of the regular season so that he could "rest up" for the LCS against the Cincinnati Red-Legs.

The reporters went nuts with the obvious, focusing on statistics only. Echoed over and over, "Roberto, what happens if you don't get your 3,000th hit because you're sitting out the last three games?" Roberto was adamant in his reply stating, "If I don't get it this year, I'll get it next year. What is the big deal?" Roberto hit a ringing double off the top of the fence in his last regular season at bat. This was definitely a *hit of fate*, if ever there was one.

Clemente showed his greatness with this focused decision to sit out. It was a clear and simple solution to the dumbfounded reporters' questions. Statistic-obsessed reporters probably "freaked out" at the notion that some great player could concentrate on what was needed to be done versus some arbitrary number of greatness. Would Clemente be any less great if he had finished with 2,999 hits? Likewise, Hall of Famer Al Kaline had 399 HRs, Lou Gehrig had *only* 493 HRs, and Mickey Mantle, who played the last two years with extremely debilitated knees, slipped from a career average over .300, to .298. If numbers were so important, Mickey had said, he "would have been the first 50-50 man [homers and steals] a couple of times."

The fair pole played a part in the 1997 World Series. Moises Alou swung at a 2 – 2 pitch from Orel Hershiser, and Bob Costas announced that, "The ball hit the foul pole for a three-run homer, giving the Marlins a 4 –1 lead." Hit the what? In 1998, Mark McGwire's 51st hit the fair pole. Can you imagine sitting with a foreign dignitary and trying to explain this "foul thing" to them?

The umpires have always had a say on this foul thing. In the 1930s, a ball hitting the foul pole was in play, not a home run!

At Comiskey Park, the foul poles were actually bent back slightly to join them at the top of the roof. In Yankee Stadium during the 1930s, a ball hitting the foul pole was in play, not a home run. In 1939, a disputed foul ball foul ball down the left field line at the Polo Grounds created an argument in which the Giants' Billy Jurges and umpire George Magerkurth spit at each other! That led National League President Ford Frick to order two-foot screens installed inside all foul poles; the American League soon followed suit.

Once, during the April 1960 Opening Day game at Los Angeles, the umpires protested on the grounds that the foul poles were actually in fair territory. In 1962 in Los Angeles, when larger and taller *fair poles* were installed (some are presently 32 feet), it was discovered that they were accidentally installed completely in foul territory. Special dispensation was rendered from the National League so that they were recognized as fair, but the next year's plate was moved so that the poles were actually fair. That sounds like a sandlot diamond to me. That's great. Let's throw the bat, choose up sides, and get on with the game.

The Montreal Expos played in the bowled Olympic Stadium. It was built to house the 1976 Olympics. The *fair poles* extended only part of the way up on the structure. Way up on the rim, 180 feet high, there were real designated markings of fair or foul.

One night, Gary Carter was watching Dave "King Kong" Kingman from the bench. Kingman is the most prolific home run hitter who will never make the Hall of Fame. He clouted *at least* 442 round trippers. I say at least because, that night, he smashed a "Mick- Like" shot, a high prodigious shot to left. It was so far up, that the umpires had to quickly confer on the ruling. They didn't have the foggiest notion whether it was fair or foul and ruled it foul. As Gary Carter told me, "It was *definitely* fair."

After the season, Montreal spent a large sum of money to extend the *fair line* through the different tiers and rim. Huge cranes had to be brought in to perform the task. Lo and behold, Gary Carter soon thereafter saw a young Darryl Strawberry of the Mets hit the rim in right, a mighty shot of 180 feet high, near the line, and it was ruled fair. Darryl also hit one off the fair pole in the 1999 ALC in Boston while playing for the Yankees.

In 1998, Chicago White Sox slugger Frank Thomas hit a terrific home run in Tampa, off their knuckleballer Dennis Springer. It left the park high over the fair pole and hit a catwalk that extended off the roof of the stadium. Because it was such an exceptional shot, the umpires ruled that it was a homer versus playing the ball as it lands in a domed stadium. A month later, another ball hit the catwalk and was ruled a double! Amazingly, in 1999, Paul Sorrento of the Marlins hit two consecutive foul balls backward off the catwalk. Mike Piazza, the Mets catcher, went back for a possible play on the first one, and the ball never came down. The second one ricocheted in front of John Olerud, the first baseman for the Mets. But in Thomas's case, the call was not only a ground rule interpretation, but also a judgment call. McGwire's 66th home run (of 70) was a similar situation. In 1999, instant reply was used by umpire Frank Pulli, correctly calling a double for Florida's Cliff Floyd, but the league officials quickly balked at that. When was the last time that a ball bounced over the fence without fan interference and the umpire ruled it a triple because in his judgment the runner would have made three bases? Or how about the possibility of a runner not being able to make second base with the new parks being so ridiculously small and the umpire awarding him only one base?

Umpires' judgment has come into play in many other ground rule situations, too, but in the old days at Wrigley Field, the playing rules were quite unique. A ball going into the ivy was in play. The fielder had to fish it out and fire it back in as the runners circled the bases.

Ralph Kiner, former National League home run king and outfielder, said as a Mets broadcaster, "I used to hide a ball or two in strategic spots. If I couldn't find the hit baseball, I'd quickly go and retrieve my hidden one. It looked a little puzzling when I ran 10 to 12 feet away from where the ball went into the ivy and I came out with *the* ball, but that's what we did."

In 1974, Mike Schmidt, Philadelphia's great Hall of Fame slugging third baseman, blasted a shot off the speaker at the

Houston Astrodome and was credited with a "prodigious single." The ball hit the public-address speaker 117 feet up and 329 feet from home plate and would have traveled 500 feet but dropped into center field. At least it wasn't called foul.

Baseball has been groping to make positive changes and reconnect with old fans. The Baseball Gods are messing around with the precious natural elements of the game, where the sun is shining, the grass is green, the crack of the bat is euphoric and distinct versus a silly *ping*, and the ball can take a bad hop off a stone or the lip of the infield and create *a play of fate.*

By changing the fair line to the correct nomenclature, the Baseball Gods would help with the long overdue interpretation of a very basic rule. But more than that, it would pay respect to one of the basic elements of a beautiful, simplistic game.

7

PLAYS OF FATE

One day, I had lunch at Mamasan's, a Thai and Vietnamese restaurant in Rochester, with a business associate. After lunch, I squeezed by the table next to us. My foot inadvertently hooked a young lady's purse strap near the floor. I dragged it for another step. We looked at each other, and I quickly responded to the situation by saying, "Oh no, you caught me!" We laughed, and I exited.

As soon as I was outside, I remembered that I had left my briefcase under my table. I rushed back in. Upon passing the young lady again, I said, "I think tripping over your purse was fate because I was being told not to leave without my briefcase."

I quickly grabbed my briefcase and was next to my new friend again. I looked at her once more and merely said, "Good thing I remembered that I forgot!"

So, what is a "play of fate"? How can it be known for sure that this play wasn't merely a break of the game? What is perplexing is that a play of fate can go along with a historical trend. These include the Yankees Dynasty with Jeffrey Maier reaching over the railing, the Celtics' mystique with John Havlicek or Larry Bird. However, a play of fate could go against tradition, like the 1969 Mets and Jets.

With reference to the criterion, a play of fate must involve real baseball fans who possess a profound understanding of the "inner game" of baseball. The play must also have two clearly polarized outcomes:

1. One fan will experience a gut-wrenching feeling of nausea in the pit of his or her stomach.
2. At the same time, another fan will experience the feeling of exuberant jubilation. Most often, the negatively impacted fan will be the one to bring up the play, rather than the beneficiary. The loser will often verbalize his or her complaint, still not believing just how unfortunate the team was, whereas the winner will merely smile. I certainly don't go around bragging about Bucky Dent's home run, but Red Sox fans just keep dwelling on it. As far as the effect on both sides, our magnificent game of baseball usually has perfect balance.

I first became fully aware of a real play of fate when I was 11. It was late in the seventh game of the 1960 World Series between the Pirates and the Yankees. My transistor radio was stuck to my ear so that I could hear each important out. The Yankees were up 7 – 4 in the beginning of the inning, but the Pirates opened with a single by Gino Cimoli. I started to pray for a ground ball.

Suddenly the announcer said, "Virdon hits a ground ball towards short." Yes! That's it, we've got it! All of a sudden, the ball took a bad hop and hit Kubek in the throat. For a second, I wasn't sure if Tony had made the play or not, but I was still hoping. A split second later, the announcer clarified that Kubek was down after getting hit in the "Adam's Apple," and there was no play.

At *that* moment, I had the impending feeling of doom! I still tried to believe that that play was an isolated incident and would not turn the tide. But at just 11 years old, I was already aware of what a play of fate could be.

*

Many famous plays of fate have occurred since Harry Frazee traded Babe Ruth from the Red Sox to the Yankees. Those plays didn't work out so well for Fred "Bonehead" Merkle, Fred Snodgrass, Johnny Pesky, Mickey Owens, Ralph Terry, Bill Buckner, and Ralph Branca. Some of the noted winners, however, were Enos Slaughter, Bill Mazeroski, Bucky Dent, and Bobby Thomson.

Ralph Branca was a very good pitcher at the beginning of his career, winning 21 games in 1947. He hurt his arm a little after that but was still a respectable going 14 – 9, 13 – 5, and then slipping to 7 – 9 in 1950. In 1951, the year that the Dodgers had a 14-game lead on the Giants, Branca gave up the "shot that was heard around the world." He was 13 – 12 for the season. His lifetime ERA is a decent 3.79.

Ralph was one of those good guys who did finish last, in a sense, for much too long. His life was never the same, after Bobby Thomson's homer, for many years to come. People would only label him as a loser, not the good athlete and person he was – just like Bill Buckner, who could not show his face in Beantown for some time.

Finally, after seeking professional advice, Ralph Branca turned his life around. A psychologist told him that until he joined the people instead of going against the people's perception, nothing would change. Wisely, he called up Bobby Thomson, and they started to do road shows together. Branca started joking that he made Thomson famous. "What the hell," he said. "I had a bad month. I got married that month, too!" (Maybe it was due to El Niño!) The audiences then roared with delight, and Branca was finally at ease with himself. Does Bill Buckner need Mookie Wilson's phone number?

When we were kids, we often heard the old adage, "The faster they come in, the further they go out." Actually, the physics of the game dictate that "The faster they come in, the faster they go out," taking the energy of the ball and reversing the direction with the inertia of the bat. Sometimes this speed creates a terrible situation.

Herb Score was the potential equal of Sandy Koufax or Nolan Ryan. He was a starting southpaw pitcher with Cleveland in 1955. In his first two years, he was 16 – 10 and 20 – 9. He led the league each year in strikeouts with 245 and 263 respectively. In 1952 in the minors, he struck out 330 batters in 251 innings. In 1955, he was the Rookie of the Year in the American League. In 1956, he led the league in shutouts with five. He struck out 15 Senators in one game and was also the winning All-Star pitcher. He was 23 years old and "hot stuff."

On May 7, 1957, Gil McDougald, who was also a previous Rookie of the Year New York Yankee's infielder, used a pronounced open stance. He hit a wicked line drive that struck

Herb Score in the right eye. Score was carried off the field on a stretcher, with a broken nose and lacerations.

Score returned to the mound the next year, but he never fully regained his form. Please don't ask me where the balance was there. Score claimed that he was effective in spring training of the next year, but soon thereafter, he hurt his arm and didn't tell anyone. "These are the mistakes you make when you are young," he commented. Gil McDougald was devastated by this experience and retired at 32 years old.

One must believe that the home run that Cleveland's Sandy Alomar, Jr., struck off Yankees pitcher Mariano Rivera in the 1997 Divisional Series was a "hit of fate." For fellow Yankees fans, I was livid when Yankees manager Joe Torre took out pitcher Mike Stanton. What bothers me to no end are statistical match-ups. Stanton had just made Dave Justice, who was a beautiful, pure hitter, look foolish. Stanton had his range, timing, and confidence and had just thrown six unhittable strikes to two batters. The ball was coming through the strike zone at the ultimate slinging angle, just as Dennis Eckersley could do from the right side, in his prime. So, you take him out just because righty Matt Williams was up next? Besides, why not bring in Ramiro Mendoza in the eighth inning in their "natural order?" (Rivera to close.) Surely, as I was having this real-time discussion with my son, Adam, other real Yankees fans were, too.

Furthermore, anyone who believes in scrapping and playing "little ball" when "all the chips are down" would most likely implore Derek Jeter to bunt in the first inning of Game Seven with Tim Raines at second base and no outs. Jeter struck out swinging, holding Raines. Paul O'Neill hit a grounder to first that would have surely scored Raines from third. Naturally, the Yankees squandered a run here and there when it was time to play "inside ball" and lost by one run. Where have you gone, Mugsy McGraw?

Was all this supposed to happen because it was Sandy Alomar's year? He started with an impressive 30-game hitting streak and game-winning All-Star home run in his own park and ended with clutch performances against the Yankees, Orioles, and Marlins. Although his team lost to the Marlins in seven games, he brought balance, in terms of pride and class, to his family. Sandy lightened the load of his brother Robbie's despicable action against umpire John Hirschbeck.

Clemente's last hit was clearly a hit of fate. So was Ted Williams's last at bat, producing homer number 521, as it sailed through the cold and bitter autumn gust of wind into the Fenway stands. Was Roger Maris's 61st home run a hit of fate? I can only argue that records are made to be broken, and it was fate that he was let down gently by a Yankee before this new manufactured condition allows many to enhance their production. Remember that Babe had also lost his World Series scoreless inning pitching streak to Yankee pitcher Whitey Ford with 32 in 1961. Ruth's record had held up for nearly four decades.

If Mark McGwire's feat of 1998 was meant to be, and Sammy Sosa, too, surpassing 61 homers, it was only for the purpose of finally seeing Roger Maris gets the well-deserved acclaim and overdue election into the Hall of Fame.

In 2004, the Red Sox broke the jinx with the Yankees, up three games to two. One play in particular was indicative of a "real" play of fate. In the 14-inning game against Boston, Tony Clark hit a ground rule, pinch-hit double that bounced and hit the seat railing from the underside. If the ball had caught under the rail half an inch more, it would have stayed in play, and Ruben Sierra would have scored. The Yankees' momentum would have ended the drama. But that's not always the way the ball bounces!

The big question is: can you possibly stop a play of fate? The answer is unmistakably *no*. The beauty of baseball is that many true fans have had the experience firsthand as players or coaches. Reflecting back, everyone has had a momentary premonition of the future that turned out precisely as predicted. Forget all this outlandish statistical analysis. The game is not played on a chart or graph -- or like football, which has a clock and adds a manipulative aspect to the sport.

My best personal experience with a shocking play of fate is as follows. It was a "coach's dream" to coach my daughter, Lauren's Senior League Softball team. We were loaded with talent and started the season off with a 7 – 0 record.

But one young lady on the team had her own agenda ever since she had walked onto the practice field on day one. She had just been cut from the junior varsity team the day before and just wasn't going to listen or change.

In the eighth game, we were up by three runs and rolling along. But soon a left-hander was up for the other team. I implored my young friend to move three feet closer to the bag at third base line.

I said, "She's not going to be able to get around and will hit the ball exactly between where you are standing and the bag."

She refused to move. Two pitches, no swings. Again, I demanded that she move over. She very reluctantly moved over about 15 inches. Naturally, the next pitch was ripped exactly where I predicted: on the line. She reached out and the ball caromed off the end of her mitt! At this point, it appeared as a harmless single, but I knew better.

I looked over to another coach and quietly whispered, "I bet that we'll lose this game by one run!"

"No," he said.

"Yes," I answered, followed by my brash clairvoyant response. "I've just been around the game too long." He just couldn't believe it. Neither could I; I had never thought nor said anything like it before. What a shame it was. We were looking forward to a once-in-a-lifetime undefeated season. With two outs, the other team scored five runs. We uncharacteristically threw the ball to the wrong spots and made physical errors, too.

When we finally got our ups, we promptly started a nice rally. With one out, one run in, and a runner on first, the next batter hit a clean single to right-center. Our runner from first cruised into third where I was coaching. I yelled, "Stop here!" with both arms up, as the ball was already back on the edge of the outfield grass. For some strange reason, for the first time that year one of the very good listeners ran for home and was tagged out by 15 feet. Two outs. The next batter lined out on a remarkable defensive play, one of those once-in-a-lifetime efforts by the other team's weakest player.

We lost that game by one run. Overall, we finished the season with three losses by a grand total of three runs!

I'm sure that all real baseball fans have had their own experience of a play of fate. For those skeptics who do not really understand baseball anyway, I ask, "Why wasn't I able to stop the outcome?" I yelled to position my third baseman as clearly as my base runner. The answer is simply that it was a "play of fate" and just meant to be. Just because I saw it coming doesn't mean that I could change it. Who do you think I am, the supernatural Satchel Paige?

The balance in this situation is clear. I reminded each and every one of these very talented kids of something that they needed to understand. Just because that they could dominate in this league, the competition is always keener at the next level. They needed to stay hungry to progress.

They say that in each adverse event there is a silver lining. The next three years started a wonderful progression on the bitter lesson that we learned.

Our shortstop became a four-year varsity starter, and two of our pitchers became four-year varsity starters, splitting the assignment. The other pitcher became a five-year varsity starter, as we have two high schools. Our catcher became a five-year varsity starter and was named first string All-County as a freshman!

Our third baseman retired.

*

The first of my three biggest "plays of fate" was when I ran out of elementary school in October 1960 only to hear that Bill Virdon had hit Tony Kubek in the throat. On May 22, 1963, the second play of fate occurred with Mickey Mantle's most impressive and hardest-hit home run ever. But this play of fate wasn't just about the game. It also had to do with the events that led up to me turning on my bedroom radio, just three seconds before Mickey's home run.

If you believe no other stories in this book, please believe this one.

Wednesday, May 22 was the first balmy night of the spring in 1963. That was the first night that I ever went anywhere with Garry Hurwitz without his brother Mark, my first and life-time friend. We went to the JYMA in Rochester on Andrews Street to play basketball.

Garry was almost two years older than me. I was exactly 14 years and three months old on that night. Garry had just turned 16 the previous week. He was only one grade ahead of me because I started school at four years old. His brother Mark, my best friend, was in my class. Garry and Mark lived in the house right behind mine, with no fence between our yards.

That night, Garry and I took the city bus up and back to the gym. Garry and I had no trouble further bonding and had a good time playing basketball.

Coming back, we exited the bus near home, Garry was on the higher step just behind me. Suddenly, he "flicked" my ear as we were hitting the sidewalk, which was a common practice during that stage of our lives. Then he attempted to do it again and again, and I deflected his hand on both attempts. I wouldn't put up with his nonsense and started to sprint ahead, a few yards or so, up the two blocks that we had to go.

At this point in my life, I was just beginning to get out of my husky Yogi-like stage and was gaining some speed for the first time. Garry, on the other hand, had always had a much slimmer build at about 5'10" and 145 pounds or less, and he was much faster.

Garry was catching up to me, but I was determined not to let him "flick" my ear again because that hurt, but more importantly, ear flicks were psychologically demeaning. No "man" would take that without a battle. I could hear his feet just one-half stride behind me. He reached out and grazed my shoulder. I ran faster. Yet again, Garry nearly had me in his grasp. I sped up as if I was in a "run-down," with two outs in the bottom of the ninth.

We were both laughing and really beginning to enjoy this strange camaraderie! I kept sprinting faster than I had ever sprinted in my life! This exercise continued nearly all the way back to his yard before he gave up! We were in high spirits and laughing loudly upon entering the far end of his circular driveway. The usual 10-minute walk from the bus stop most certainly took under one-half that time. Our race marked the beginning of an era of new respect.

Above us, Mark yelled out of his upstairs bedroom window: "Bob, if you hurry you can hear Mickey's at bat!"

Mark's voice caught me off guard. I yelled, "What?"

Mark yelled, "Hurry! Mickey's up! If you peel, you can catch him!"

I took off like a shot. Thank God, I was all warmed up! I estimated that it would take me no more than 15 seconds to get through the front door of my house, run down the short hall, and turn on the radio in my bedroom.

Suddenly, I had the clearest premonition of my baseball life. *If Mickey is batting left-handed, he is going to hit one.* It was so clear that I sort of verbalized it. Mickey had hit many a lofty, left-handed "Ruthian" shot, but I lived to see him swing from the right side, with that raw power like nobody else had ever displayed.

My father instantly saw me tear in and down the hall. Streaking past, I simply yelled "Mickey's up!" He understood.

My radio was on in a flash and of course already tuned to the right station. The first words I heard were, "The right-hander is rubbing up the ball!"

I cringed, smiled, and said, "Oh my God." I couldn't believe that the announcer would even say that, and at this exact moment in my life! Most often, announcers would refer to "the pitcher" or use his name. That right-hander was Bill Fischer of the Kansas City A's.

Next came the words that I have the clearest recollection of in my life:

"Mantle swings and that ball is gone and is still raising! I think it is out of Yankee Stadium! Oh my God, I think it is

OUT OF THE STADIUM…. then it finally it hit the facade with a tremendously audible ringing *thud* just below the top of the facade!"

I sat on my bed with tears of awe. Mickey had hit the ball so hard and the ball flew so fast that it would have left the park if Yankee Stadium had been built just a foot or two deeper. The ball traveled nearly 400 feet away and soared almost 120 feet high before hitting the facade with a BOOM as they heard at Gettysburg.

After a few minutes of listening to the cheers, I suddenly got a different feeling. I was pissed that the ball hadn't flown out. I was aware of that possibility because this was now the second time the ball had hit the facade. Mark and I often debated if was even humanly possible to hit a ball out of Yankee Stadium, and my conclusion was that *only* Mickey could do it!

What a chain of events! I heard the longest home run in the history of baseball live, and Mickey was the one to hit it!

And thank you Garry, for flicking my ear for the last time ever.

*

My third and most important "play of fate" occurred on New Year's Eve 1966 when I met my lovely wife and soulmate, Jill.

Throughout the last week of 1966, my dear friend Rik Karchefsky twisted my arm to attend a New Year's Eve party. After much prodding, I agreed to get fixed up on a "trial" date first. I didn't want to partake in either. Reluctantly, I went on a trial date during the week and then to the New Year's Eve party.

I rode to the party in another friend's 1965 Chevy convertible, yellow with a white top. We picked up his date first – a casual relationship, in his mind.

Lo and behold, we parked in the driveway, and I watched Jill walk out on her porch. Oh my God, I saw an aura around her!

At the party that night, I told a joke, and Jill was the only one who laughed.

We dated for five years and have been very happily married for 47 years. How was telling that joke not a play of fate? Thank you Rik!

8

BASEBALL PLAYERS ARE SUPERSTITIOUS

On August 14, 1969, the Cubs had an eight-and-a-half-game lead over the Cardinals and a nine-and-a-half-game lead over the Mets. Playing the Mets, the Cubs were about ready to clinch their first postseason spot since the World Series of 1945.

On that infamous day in baseball history, a black cat walked onto the field and over to the edge of the Mets dugout. It hesitated there for a moment and then proceeded across the field to the Cubs dugout.

The rest is history. The Cubs lost out to the Mets for the season. Would the black cat ever return and jinx the opponent?

Spend enough time studying the game of baseball and its players, and you're bound to hear at least one of these "rules" of the game:

Don't step on that foul line as you leave fair territory. Wear the same cap for the remainder of the season, whether you get lice or not. Wear the same the same T-shirt with a hole in it. Eat in the same restaurant and order the same food from the same waitress, sitting at the same table, for as long as you're in a hot streak. Don't step on the "fair line." Travel to the ballpark using the exact same route at the exact same time. Put on the same shoe first. Wear the same stinky batting glove. Sit in the same spot on the dugout stairs. Spit on the same concrete slab. Go up the dugout stairs one at a time. Throw your water cup down in the exact same spot. Take exactly the same number of practice swings when you're in the batter's box. Hold the label away from you in the exact same manner, each at bat.

Some players have held tight to their own superstitions: eat your chicken every day (Wade Boggs); eat tacos before every start (Justin Verlander); brush your teeth after eating black licorice following each half of an inning (Turk Wendell).

Whatever you do, don't ever admit that you're in a slump… or wear the number 13!

(One time, when Roger Craig had lost 20 games for the Mets, he considered changing his number to 13 -- anything to break a curse!)

A special remembrance goes out to the passing of Mr. Ralph Theodore Joseph "Hawk" Branca, who was wearing *lucky* number 13 on his back when he delivered that infamous last pitch to Bobby Thomson, in the ninth inning of the third and last game of the playoff series. I can still hear announcer Russ Hodges shouting, "And the Giants win the pennant! And the Giants win the Pennant! And the Giants win the Pennant!"

Ralph Branca was a wonderful man and darn good pitcher. When Jackie Robinson made his Major League debut on Opening Day 1947, Branca stood beside Robinson when all other players had refused to. Branca won 80 games for the Brooklyn Dodgers, 21 of which occurred that same year. He led the league in wins in 1948 and in won-lost percentage in 1949.

Since his mother was Jewish, I can definitely say that Ralph was a real *mensch*!

P.S. In 1984, a black cat walked onto the field when the Cubs were playing the Phillies. This time, the cat stopped at the Cubs dugout and then proceeded across to the Phillies dugout and walked in. The Cubs finally won their division! In 2016, the black cat passed away. The beloved Cubs won another World Series against the Indians -- the first since 1908!

9

NICE GUYS FINISH LAST?

During the drafts of Little League, Senior League, and Big League Hardball and Softball seasons, I would always take decent ball players who were nice kids. Invariably, early during each season, I would have to firmly remind them that they must be more intense on the field if they were to compete and win. Do nice guys really finish last?

Whoever made up the expression that "nice guys finish last"?

Leo Durocher, the scrappy shortstop for the Brooklyn Dodgers who later became their manager, claimed to have coined it. "Giants, led by Mel Ott, began to come out of their dugout to take their warm-ups," Durocher recalled in his memoir, *Nice Guys Finish Last*. "Without missing a beat I said, 'Take a look at Number Four (Ott) there. A nicer guy never drew a breath than that man there.' I called off his players' names as they came marching up the steps behind him, 'Walker, Cooper, Mize, Kerr, Gordon, Thomson. Take a look at them. All nice guys. They'll finish last. Nice guys. Finish last.'" Some baseball historians have refuted the origin of the expression. Regardless of its true origin, this quote embodied Leo's crusty disposition.

As a manager, Durocher won a pennant in 1941 with "Dem Bums." In 1948, after eight years as Brooklyn manager, Leo shocked the by taking the helm of the archrival New York Giants in midseason. Durocher was suspended a year earlier by Branch Rickey, for "alleged conduct unbecoming the game." Durocher was a "bad apple."

In the Brooklyn community, he was losing his popularity soon after he divorced the popular actress Lorraine Day. The local Catholic Youth Organization withdrew its support of the Knothole Club because "Durocher has undermined the moral training of Brooklyn's Roman Catholic youths." "Leo the Lip" was at the helm to lead the Giants to the pennant in 1951, when Bobby Thomson hit "the shot heard 'round the world." Durocher also managed rookie Willie Mays in 1951. He was still the manager in 1954, when Mays made his spectacular catch – "The Catch" – against the Cleveland Indians. Leo was tough and loved winning. He enjoyed early success, as a rookie teammate of Babe Ruth's, on the great 1927 Yankee team (although he didn't play in the '27 Series). Durocher and Ruth were also on the great Yankee teams of 1928 and 1929. The Yankees swept the Pirates in the '27 Series, beat the Cardinals in the '28 Series, and had to settle for winning only the 1929 American League pennant.

In *Nice Guys Finish Last,* Leo portrays himself as the "All-American Out," but his fielding and his attitude ("Show me a good loser, and I'll show you an idiot") won ball games. It was the great Babe "Bambino" Ruth himself who gave him the "All-American Out" nickname. Some called him spunky and irascible. He was a junkyard dog scrap fighter of a bygone era.

Not only was it his size (5'8", 160 pounds) that drove him to survive, but it was also his learning during a rough-tough era of baseball and the lingering influence of John McGraw and Miller Huggins.

Miller Huggins, who became a famous Yankee manager in Ruth's era, played as an undersized (5'6", 135 pounds) and yet marvelous infielder himself. He learned the game when the 1901 Orioles prevailed, with the infamous John J. McGraw at the helm. Late in 1917, Yankees owners Jake Ruppert and Til Huston wanted to hire "Uncle Robbie," the great '01 Orioles manager Wilbert Robinson, who was 50 years old, but they thought of him as too old. After they met Huggins, they were impressed with his baseball genius and finally lured him into signing a two-year contract. "Mighty Mite" Huggins was well experienced when Leo came along.

"Huggins, my first manager, brought me up, and taught me… 'I come to play! I come to win! I come to kill!'" Durocher said. The team was modeled itself off of the 1901 Orioles, led by the "rough and unruly" John "Mugsy" McGraw and Uncle Robbie.

McGraw and Robinson were known for sharpening their skills of "inside baseball," which was a very physically intimidating style of play. They perfected the hit and run, the double steal, cutting corners when the umpire was not looking, diving into the first baseman long after he had caught the ball, banging into runners on defense and throwing masks in front of home plate.

The Orioles of the 1890s, as a whole, were not a bunch of nice guys, but they did win at a regular pace due to their intimidation and hard-nosed style of play. "At Chattanooga, McGraw, playing shortstop, held a runner by the belt to keep him from advancing on a fly ball, spiked the opposing shortstop sliding into second, and slapped a sliding Chattanooga runner in the face with the ball, bloodying his nose," Durocher said in *Nice Guys Finish Last*.

In July of 1902, McGraw was named the manager of the Giants, a post he would hold for 30 years. McGraw was an enigma in his own time. In 1908, a Chicago writer described him as "Having a Jekyll-and-Hyde personality: in uniform he was the 'incarnation of rowdyism, the personification of meanness and howling blatancy'; off the field he was the kindest, most generous and most sympathetic of men." But others, Durocher said, saw him off the field as, "thoughtless, surly and belligerent, particularly on those not- uncommon occasions when he had too much to drink."

Leo Durocher was also the shortstop for St. Louis's "Gashouse Gang," which emulated McGraw's style of play. They were considered "the roughest, rowdiest, most colorful team ever." Leo admitted that he would sharpen his belt buckle and nick the ball in key situations. Leo believed in having rules, only because, "If there weren't any rules, how could I break them?"

But do ball players need to follow the personas McGraw, Robinson, Huggins, and Durocher to win? Maybe it will work for some, but there are unique personalities that are "tough as nails" on the field with a different personality in real life.

When you met the late Hank Bauer, the outstanding outfielder of the New York Yankees in the 1950s, it was quite obvious that he was a fine gentleman. He possessed the rare talent of being tough as they come on the field, without needing a "bush league" style of play, and authentically a nice guy off the field. For those who might question whether Bauer mellowed out after his playing career, approach the question with one basic thought: rarely, if ever, does human nature change. Durocher never mellowed out. In 1962, after a long career, Durocher was the Dodger coach and contested a "foul" call by umpire Jocko Conlan. As Durocher himself explains, "Sure I kicked dirt on him and then he kicked me in the shins. I kicked him in the shins, he kicked me back, and I kicked him again."

History proves that Hank Bauer always maintained this marvelous unique blend of tenacity and being a gentleman. Bauer was an ex- Marine who earned two Purple Hearts and then joined the Yankees late in 1948. He played just 19 games at the end of the season. It is no coincidence that Hank's stay coincided with the start in 1949 of a record five World Series wins in a row for New York Yankees manager Casey Stengel and eleven of Hank's teammates. Hank was "Charlie Hustle" before Pete Rose. It was Bauer you would see running to first on a walk, sliding head first, and vigorously breaking up a double play before Pete Rose played. He had a great work ethic, which Casey loved. He also had a strong, accurate arm. Bauer said, "I could throw with Carl Furillo," the very strong-armed Brooklyn right-fielder.

When Hank was a rookie, and for many years after, he had speedy legs and the ultimate hustle. One day, after getting an excellent jump on a ball, he made a fine running catch in right-center field. Joe DiMaggio promptly told him to stay in his own territory. Hank never quit on the field. He amassed nine AL championships and seven world championships in 12 years.

When "the chips were down," Bauer was at his best. Hank was the original "Mr. October" and "Mr. Clutch" long before Reggie Jackson. He still holds the pure World Series record of hitting in 17 straight games (not just post-season play). Hank admitted that Roberto Clemente had been likely to break his record if he hadn't tragically been killed. Marquis Grissom made a good pass at the record, with a streak of 15 games. Hank reflected his feelings during our conversation saying, "Even if someone does break it, I've held this for at least 40 years." His 46 series hits still rank him high up on the list all time, but way behind the incredible Yogi Berra's 71. But, as usual, statistics only tell a small part of the real story.

In Game Six of the 1951 Series, with a hard-fought battle against the New York Giants, the game was tied 1 – 1 in the bottom of the sixth inning. Bauer came up with the bases loaded and drove a triple to deep left, clearing the bases. In the Giants' ninth inning and down 4 – 1, Alvin Dark, Whitey Lockman, and Eddie Stanky ("The Brat," who was not perceived as a nice guy, although Tommy John really liked playing for him in Chicago) singled to load the bases. "The Old Professor" Casey Stengel astonished everyone by bringing in lefty Bob Kuzava to pitch to right-handed slugger Monte Irvin. Irvin drove the ball deep to left, and Gene Woodling made the play. All three runners tagged-up and advanced. Bobby Thomson, the great playoff hero, drove another ball deep to left, and Al Dark scored after the catch. Pinch-hitter Sal Yvars then sliced a low liner to the right, which looked like a game-tying hit. But Hank Bauer made a fantastic diving catch, grabbing the ball just inches off the ground. Hank bestowed a Ph.D. on Casey's "Professor" moniker.

In Game Three of the 1958 Series, against the World Champion Milwaukee Braves, the Yankees were down two games to zero, with Warren Spahn and Lew Burdette again spinning their magic, as Bauer came up big again. He drove in all four runs for the Yankees with a two-run single and a two-run homer. His heroics allowed the Yankees to eventually come back from a 3 – 1 game deficit against a very talented Braves ball club.

Undoubtedly, Bauer was a winner of major proportions. He was intense but maintained his cool-headed perspective even when Casey platooned him with Gene Woodling in right field. Naturally, he would get mad at Casey because he wanted to play, which was understandable, but Hank never swore to his face or spit at anyone.

Because of Bauer's fine skills, desire, and productivity, he very modestly said that he would have been worth $20 million to $30 million a year in today's market. I say at least that much. He was "Mr. Productivity," and *that* is what pays the big bucks. Remember that Sammy Sosa of the Cubs made nearly $18 million in 2005! I'll still take Hank 10 country miles ahead of Sammy to make for a winning ball club.

Hank and his teammates would stick together all the time and discuss that game's situations for hours. His close teammates and friends were Mickey Mantle and Billy Martin. Admittedly, they did have a few beers after the games as they engaged in these conversations, just as naturally as Sosa and others scooped out creatine in their clubhouse. Later in life, Hank reaffirmed that, "Mickey didn't drink all that much until the end of his career, when his original friends like Whitey Ford, Yogi, Roger Maris, Clete Boyer, Moose Skowron, Bobby Richardson, and Tony Kubek left. Billy Martin was traded right after his birthday party, at the Copacabana, in May of 1957, which ended in a well-publicized brawl. There were some very drunk and obnoxious guys having a bowling banquet at the club. They started mouthing off to the Yankees in a big way. Bauer was ready to clock the worst offender. But he reassured me, 'I didn't hit the guy. I was going to, because they were so obnoxious and kept ridiculing us, but the bouncer beat me to it.'" Bauer was sued for $250,000, a staggering figure for those times, but was found completely innocent of all charges.

Casey and the Yankees owners, Dan Topping and Del Webb, held opposing views on drinking and this incident in particular. The owners quickly traded Billy Martin to Kansas City, and there was nothing that Casey could do, even though he loved Billy like a son. Billy, most definitely, was heartbroken, and arguably was never the same as a player. As far as having a few drinks, Casey, a Manhattan drinker himself, "didn't like milkshake drinkers because they would never feel better the next day."

Bauer won the New York Baseball Writers' Association's "Good Guy" award in 1959. That was also the year that he was traded to Kansas City along with Don Larsen, Norm Siebern, and "Marvelous Marv" Throneberry. The return package delivered Joe DeMaestri, Kent Hadley, and Roger Maris, who hit 39 for homers for the Yankees in 1960. Mickey hit 40, but Roger barely beat out Mickey for the MVP award.

It amazes me that people claim that Roger Maris was a "one-year wonder." He was an all-around terrific player for many years. He was also a great right fielder, with a gun-like, accurate arm. How can people be so ignorant and act as if they are such great authorities? Ironically, that is the beauty of baseball, the great American pastime, where each fan has the right to his or her own opinion.

Being traded to Kansas City was actually a blessing for Hank Bauer. He played for a year and a half, then he was asked by the infamous Charles O. Finley, owner of the Kansas City Athletics, to manage the team. The offer couldn't have happened to a nicer guy. But in September of 1962, Hank resigned, so Finley "wouldn't get a chance to fire me."

In 1963, Lee MacPhail hired him as coach of the Baltimore

Orioles. In 1964, Hank became their manager. He lost the pennant race to his old pal Yogi by just two games. After the 1965 season, the Orioles acquired Frank Robinson, the 1966 Triple Crown winner and MVP of the National League. Under Hank's tutelage, the Orioles went on to win the 1966 World Series. Hank was also named the Major League Manager of the Year by The Sporting News. The Series win gave Hank yet another world championship ring.

Hank proudly wore his "five-in-a-row" World Series ring to our book signing in Rochester, New York. He quickly rattled off the names of his teammates who had also earned this most coveted prize: Charley Silvera (Yogi's backup), Gene Woodling, Vic Raschi, Allie Reynolds, Ed Lopat, Phil Rizzuto, Yogi, Bobby Brown (although he was in the service in 1953), Jerry Coleman, Joe Collins, Ralph Houk, and Casey Stengel. This fact is a great trivia question for *real* Yankees fans.

At that time, Hank willingly came out to autograph shows for much less than the going price. He certainly could have commanded more. Hank graciously signed more items than were contracted for without a fuss. He also hung around baseball shows and talked baseball with fans when time permitted.

Bauer was a huge winner on the field and a huge winner in life. Other nice guys have won, too. Mickey was a nice guy with a remarkable record. Gil Hodges was a real nice guy who slipped by the Yankees once in 1955 and managed the Mets to their miracle victory over the Orioles in 1969. Brooks Robinson was a gem, and Cal Ripken became the "Ambassador of Baseball." Tony Gwynn also won the Baseball Writers' Nice Guy Award and won the Roberto Clemente Man of the Year award in 1999 for his work on the field and in the community.

Tommy John is also a superbly nice man. He often does

work for charities and delivers excellent messages to kids. He spends quality time talking about the old baseball days and is a terrific role model. He amassed 288 wins in his long and distinguished career. Someday he will be voted into the Hall of Fame. This is a real decent guy, who certainly is a winner through and through.

Bill "Moose" Skowron, once a halfback at Purdue and a great Yankee slugger, was one of the nicest guys of all time. Peter Golenbock commented that, "Skowron was an extraordinarily good-natured person." He played for the Yankees from 1954 to 1962 and more than carried his weight on the Yankees and other teams. He certainly won his share of times.

Bauer, Mantle, Hodges, Robinson, Ripken, Gwynn, John, and Skowron, along with thousands of other nice guys, didn't finish last. So, keep those words on your lip.

"PITCHERS CAN'T HIT"

"What is this, the 'Powder Puff' League?"

Who was the brilliant one who made up the baseball axiom that "pitchers can't hit"? Is it a corollary of Murphy's Law? Or was it a non-purist, money-mongering, antibaseball mind that started the expression? Let's let baseball's best subject, Babe Ruth, shatter this misconception.

Babe Ruth was the finest southpaw in the American League from 1915 to 1918. He was undoubtedly the Rookie of the Year in 1915 even though the award hadn't yet been created. Babe was the best pitcher in all of baseball in 1916 and 1917. He was a dominant force and was exceptional when the competition was fiercest. The first five times that Babe faced the great Walter "Big Train" Johnson, the best pitcher in the history of the American League still in his prime, Ruth beat him.

1917 Pitching Stats								
Player	W	L	ERA	CG	IP	H	BB	Ks
Ruth	24	13	2.01	35	326.1	244	108	128
Johnson	23	16	2.30	30	326	248	68	188

Although Ruth was primarily a pitcher from 1914 to 1918, he became intrigued with hitting as time wore on. As a full-time pitcher, he had a batting average of just .302, compared to his lifetime .342 average. In 1919, he hit a then record-breaking 29 home runs.

Babe's home run aptitude would soon change the course of baseball evolution. Ty Cobb and Honus Wagner were the major offensive forces in the era just preceding Ruth's dominance as a hitter. Cobb claimed that Ruth had a great advantage from learning how to hit while being a pitcher, as nobody expected results. According to Cobb, "Ruth could just go up there and practice his stroke."

And what a stroke it was! Ruth modeled his swing after the great "Shoeless" Joe Jackson. "I decided to pick out the greatest hitter to watch and study," Babe said, "and Jackson sure was good enough for me." Soon enough, Babe began stealing all the thunder with mammoth home runs that had never been seen in our great American pastime. The Bambino was being crowned as the "Sultan of Swat."

In St. Louis on July 21, 1915, Ruth hit a monumental home run that the locals hailed as the longest ever at Sportsman Park. The blast carried over the right-field roof all the way to a car dealer's window across the street. After the game, Babe proudly posed for pictures in front of the shattered window.

Now what are the critics going to say? That Babe couldn't pitch or that he couldn't hit? The fact of the matter is that other truly great players also pitched. Ted Williams, Cap Anson, Ty Cobb, and Stan Musial pitched, as well as George Sisler, who once hit .420 and .407 and pitched 24 innings. The phenomenal Honus Wagner also pitched in official games. I suppose that they couldn't hit?

Other sluggers and talented players also "went to the hill."

Rocky Colavito was not only a great slugger, but he could pitch, too. He pitched for the Indians in 1958 and the Yankees in 1968. His lifetime record was 1 – 0 with an ERA of 0.00! How could Cleveland ever trade him to Detroit in 1959 for Harvey Kuenn? (With all due respect to Harvey, who was an excellent hitter.) No doubt, that trade started *the curse* for the Indians fans!

Wade Boggs pitched for the Yankees using his knuckleball and pitched again for Tampa Bay in 1999, after he had already accomplished 3,000 hits. I wish Mickey Mantle and Brooklyn's premier first baseman Gil Hodges, who both threw great knuckleballs, had tried it. The knuckler certainly worked quite well at the end of Jim Bouton's career. Bullpen catchers refused to warm him up because he kept hitting them in the cup, "ringing their chimes."

Matty Alou, Dan Brouthers, Jose Canseco, Hal Chase, Doc Cramer, Al Dark, Erv Dusak, David Concepción, George Kelly, the infamous John J. "Mugsy" McGraw, Paul O'Neill, and Sam Rice were also very talented hitters who officially took the mound. Mickey Mantle did once, during an October 1952 all-star game. Others included Rick Cerone, Rick Dempsey, Álvaro Espinoza, José Lima, Elrod Hendricks, and Vic Davalillo.

Special recognition goes out to the versatile Bert "Campy" Campaneris, who anchored the World Champion Oakland Athletics teams in the 1970s. He usually played shortstop, but in 1965, when the A's were still in Kansas City, Campy played each of all nine positions for one whole inning, including a full inning of pitching. César Tovar did the same in 1968 while playing for the Twins. In 2000, Scott Sheldon of the Texas Rangers put his name in the record books for this same feat.

In terms of full-time pitchers who could also hit, the

powerhouse pitcher Don Newcombe hit 15 home runs and had a lifetime average of .271. In 1955, he slugged seven homers during the season. He was as mean at bat as he was on the mound. As a hitting pitcher, he was in the elite class with just a few others.

Jack Bentley, who played in Ruth's era, had a lifetime average of .291 over a shorter career.

Red Ruffing pitched for 22 years and carried a lifetime average of .269 with an astounding 36 home runs. He also amassed 521 hits.

Wes Ferrell was about the best hitting pitcher in the game after the Babe. In 15 seasons, he totaled 329 hits and had a lifetime average of .280. He also ripped 38 home runs. In 1934, he hit a home run in the eighth inning to tie the game and hit the game-winning homer for the Red Sox in the 11th inning to beat the White Sox, while "going the distance" on the mound. His lifetime slugging percentage was an incredible .446! Of course, the Red Sox traded him, too, to the Washington Senators. Ferrell was 193 – 128 in his career for a winning percentage of .601 and played on some bad teams.

Warren Spahn was definitely one of baseball's great hitting pitchers. He swatted 35 lifetime home runs, which is the National League record and fourth-best of all time. In 1958, he became one of the few pitchers to bat .300 and also win 20 games in the same season. He was very good at making contact, and he often pinch hit, enabling the runners to move up or score.

Other interesting stories about pitchers' hitting abilities have emerged over the years. In 1973, Oakland A's manager Dick Williams prepared for the upcoming World Series by using four pitchers as pinch hitters in one game. Catfish Hunter singled, Kenny Holzman walked, Darold Knowles hit a sacrifice fly, and Vida Blue struck out. That's a cool .500 for pitchers who "cannot hit." On the contrary, Hunter was an admirable hitter, and Charles Finley paid him an extra $5,000 one season due to his hitting ability.

The late Fred Hutchinson pitched for 11 years and averaged .263. He also managed the Cincinnati Reds and Pete Rose. Undoubtedly, he gave Pete some advice on hitting.

Dave Ferris was "no easy out." He compiled a lifetime average of .250 and never hit under .209.

Don Drysdale often pinch hit for the Dodgers. He was an excellent hitter, and they played "little ball" in those years. Big Don hit 29 lifetime homers. In 1965, he was the only Dodger to hit .300. He also hit seven homers, ranking him third on the team. Vin Scully remembers Drysdale hitting fifth in the batting order at times; others claimed that he hit third or fourth.

And why shouldn't a pitcher hit up in the order if qualified? Today, the answer would be that even if a pitcher could hit, he probably couldn't run the bases and be in condition to go back out and pitch. That would be like being too much of a complete ball player! Tony LaRussa, the St. Louis Cardinal Manager, didn't "manage by the book," and typically let his pitchers hit eighth. Who wrote the damn book anyway?

Ben Chapman was an outfielder-turned-pitcher for the 1944 – 45 seasons. He was 8 – 6 on the mound and *only* hit .283 for those years. His lifetime career average was .302. In July 1932, as an outfielder, he hit three homers in a game at Yankee Stadium; amazingly, two were inside-the-park shots.

The most astounding game ever as a hitting pitcher was when Tony Cloninger, a pitcher for the Atlanta Braves, set off his own fireworks in July of 1966. Cloninger belted two grand slams in one game and had nine RBIs as well as a single. As a non-pitcher, Fernando Tatis, for the St. Louis Cardinals, hit two grand slams in one inning, which is arguably now the *most* difficult baseball record to break. If you don't believe me, you can look it up!

Interestingly, in 1966, Cloninger had slugged two homers in a game two weeks before, giving him 18 RBIs in two games. Cloninger had been taking extra batting practice under the orders of his perceptive manager, Bobby Bragan.

Jim Tobin had a streak of his own. Tobin was a first-rate hitting pitcher who played for the Pirates and Boston Braves from 1937 to 1945, finishing that year with the Detroit Tigers. In 1942, in the Boston Braves home park, Tobin hit three homers in one game. He knocked six homers that year, which was the third highest number on the team. His lifetime average was an impressive .230.

In 1957, the Yankees were losing to the Chicago White Sox by a score of 4 – 0, going into the last inning. As usual, the Bronx Bombers started a rally and loaded the bases. Moose Skowron got up and smacked a grand slam to tie the game. Pitcher Tommy Byrne was called upon by Casey to pinch hit and finished them off with a home run.

Bob Lemon was an excellent Cleveland pitcher and came up as a third baseman. He won more than 200 games, with a winning percentage over .600. He hit over .230 for his career, but more importantly, he was quite adept at "placing the ball." He had remarkable bat control. As a lefty, he could take an inside pitch and hit it just fair down the third base line, nearly at will. He also placed 37 out of the park, in fair territory.

George Brett is truly an admirable Hall of Famer with his bat, although he violated the pine tar rule. Hitting definitely runs in the family. His brother Ken, a full-time pitcher, was a real fine hitter. Quite often he would pinch hit, and successfully at that. He had three .300 seasons and a .262 average.

Rick Rhoden was also one of the best hitting pitchers of his time. He batted over .300 three times and had occasional power. So did Rick Sutcliffe, slugging a Lone Star Conference homer for the Cubs. Rhoden won the National League Silver Slugger award for pitchers three years in a row, as Tom Glavine did in 1998. In 1982, Rhoden slugged a homer and a double in the same inning. In 1987, he was the DH for the Yankees for one game. Jim Palmer of the Orioles, helped his cause on many occasions, as did his teammate Mike Flanagan.

Dave McNally hit a World Series grand slam in 1970; it was the only time a pitcher had accomplished that feat. Doc Gooden of the Mets was often found engaged in a hitting conversation in the dugout. He prided himself on his ability and would have probably held a press conference about it, if asked. At one time, he was definitely one of the most reliable pinch hitters for the Mets and just hit another homer during inter-league play, for Cleveland.

Terry Forster in 16 years had just 31 hits but an astonishing lifetime average of .397!

Gary Peters of the Chicago White Sox swung a good club, too. Tommy John remembers him hitting in the sixth and seventh spot. He had a lifetime average of .222 and often put the ball in play. He slugged 19 home runs.

Dennis Cook, who played on nine different teams, was a fine hitting pitcher with a lifetime average of .277. John Smoltz spent most of his two-decade career pitching for the Braves and also carried a mean stick.

Mike Hampton, who sold out from the Mets to the Rockies, hit five homers before the end of June. But could he ever do this in New York, pre-1977?

Madison Bumgarner is an outstanding hitter. He is so good that he wanted to enter the All-Star Classic Home Run contest. One year, he hit two homers on Opening Day against Arizona and was leading the league! There's no doubt in my mind that he is a true slugger and an incredible "money pitcher."

So, pitchers cannot hit, huh? Can you imagine saying that to Cardinals pitcher Bob Gibson? Gibson grew up as a switch-hitting catcher and shortstop. Outfielder Vada Pinson once referred to Gibson as "the meanest man alive." I would pity any man who made a statement about the lack of a pitcher's abilities and then got up to face Gibson, Drysdale, or Ol' Satchel. Call the morgue.

Gibson was a complete athlete who won nine straight Gold Gloves. His lifetime batting average was .206, with 24 homers and 13 stolen bases. He hit five home runs in a single season, twice. We all know about his 1968 1.12 ERA, which was the third lowest in history behind Dutch Leonard (.96) and Mordecai "Three Fingers" Brown (1.04).

In part, the problem that we have today is that we pay players and incentivize them to become less than full athletes. The old timers could play the game the way it was meant to be played. George Uhle hit .289 over a 16-year career. Cy Young had 623 hits, Walter Johnson had 547, Bucky Walters had 477, Bob Smith of the Braves had 409, Red Lucas had 404, George Mullen had 401 and a .262 batting average, Grover Alexander had 378, Early Wynn had 365 and 300 wins, and Steve "Lefty" Carlton had 346 hits.

Lynwood "Schoolboy" Rowe was as big as the mighty Hank Greenberg but hit right-handed. During three games in 1934, he singled in the deciding run in the ninth inning. For the season, he hit .303, with 11 extra base hits and 22 runs batted in out of only 109 official at bats. Maybe opponents were walking him intentionally or "pitching around" him. In 1935, Rowe hit .312, with three home runs and 28 RBs. In 1943, as a Phillie, he led the league in both pinch hits and appearances, going 15 for 49, which is .300. Rowe had a lifetime average of .265.

Today, in this newfangled game of baseball, with all the statistics and match-ups, there are too many specialists. These overvalued specialists get too much acclaim and way too much money for being able to merely hit a "Baltimore Chop" on artificial turfs that are as hard as a rock. Others become adept at hitting "Chinese Homers" in cookie cutter stadiums that have fences as short as the miniskirts of the sixties, and rarely with the wind blowing in. Others become *spectacular* fielders, very rarely getting a bad hop off a real infield and can now bounce the ball to first base. Now we even hit for the pitcher. What in heaven's name are we doing to this game?

The next thing unsophisticated baseball fans will say is that pitchers cannot be the Most Valuable Players of the league. Who made up that one, Ford Frick?

11

PITCHERS WHO HAVE WON THE MVP AWARD

When you read the MVP votes, real baseball fans always have a definite opinion and think that they can do better, just like filling out the line-up or making trades. Here is your big chance.

At this point in the book, I hope baseball fans will at least ask which pitchers have won the Most Valuable Player Award and whether they were worth this honor. A pitcher may truly be the most value to his team each year and circumstance, versus a non-pitcher, making him a candidate for the League's MVP. However, I do believe that a pitcher should have outstanding credentials because he will play less than the non-pitcher.

When evaluating MVPs, I give some weight to the player on the winning team. This weight is in the magnitude of a tiebreaker. The reason for this weighted edge is the fact that winning on the field is often a better measurement of value than a retrospective statistical analysis. Winning tends to make up for the shortcoming of statistics.

The MVP Award was called the Chalmers Award from 1911 to 1914. Before 1910, president and general manager of the Chalmers Motor Company Hugh Chalmers presented a Chalmers Model 30 automobile to the Major League players who held the highest batting averages. However, this soon turned into a travesty.

In 1910, the batting race between Ty Cobb of the Detroit Tigers and Nap Lajoie of the Cleveland Indians turned ugly. Cobb sat out of the final game of the season to preserve his .376 batting average. But that same day, Lajoie, playing against the St. Louis Browns, managed to surpass Cobb's record with six "gimme" bunt singles. In the end, Cobb was declared batting champion due to a discrepancy in his stats. Hugh Chalmers, in turn, awarded both players with Model 30s.

In 1911, Hugh Chalmers created the Chalmers Award. Decided on by a committee of baseball writers, the Chalmers Award would go to one player in each league who could "prove himself as the most important and useful player to his club and to the league at large in point of deportment and value of services rendered." Further, there was no stipulation for the number of at-bat players needed, including pitchers; therefore, all players were eligible for the award.

With this, the language and criteria for a Most Valuable Player was adopted for future considerations. From 1915 to 1921, however, there were no awards given. That was too bad for the great Bambino. Ruth would have undoubtedly won three more MVP Awards.

Between 1922 and 1929, the MVP Award was called The League Award. Since 1931, the most valuable player has been awarded the Baseball Writers' Association of America Award.

All combined, 25 pitchers have won the MVP Award, and

17 pitchers have placed second in the balloting. Five of those times, pitchers placed second to pitchers.

Below is a list of pitchers who were named MVP, along with their stats and my analysis of the MVP choice. (**Bold** denotes league leader; * denotes pennant winner.)

1913: Walter Johnson, RHP, Washington Senators (AL)

W	L	Pct	GS	CG	IP	H	BB	Ks	ShO	ERA
36	7	**.837**	**36**	**29**	**346**	232	38	**243**	**11**	**1.14**

Definite MVP. No help from a team with a meager .252 batting average. How dare Walter walk 38 men in an amazing 346 innings? Earl Weaver would have pulled him.

1924: Walter Johnson, RHP, Washington Senators* (AL)

W	L	Pct	GS	CG	IP	H	BB	Ks	ShO	ERA
23	7	.767	38	20	278	233	77	**158**	6	**2.72**

Not the true MVP. No player could be named twice for the League Award, otherwise Babe Ruth would have won for the second year in a row – despite Washington's pennant win.

1924: Dazzy Vance, RHP, Brooklyn Robins (Dodgers) (NL)

W	L	Pct	GS	CG	IP	H	BB	Ks	ShO	ERA
28	6	.824	34	**30**	308	238	77	**262**	3	**2.16**

Not the true MVP. Rogers Hornsby of the St. Louis Cardinals had the highest batting average (.424) this century! No pennant win for Vance, either. You must be kidding!

1931: Robert Moses "Lefty" Grove, LHP, Philadelphia Athletics* (AL)

W	L	Pct	GS	CG	IP	H	BB	Ks	ShO	ERA
31	4	**.886**	30	**27**	289	249	62	**175**	4	**2.06**

Not the true MVP. Lou Gehrig had the second highest RBI total (185) in history. Gehrig ties or edges out Babe Ruth, who led that season with 46 home runs.

1933: Carl Hubbell, LHP, New York Giants* (NL)

W	L	Pct	GS	CG	IP	H	BB	Ks	ShO	ERA
23	12	.657	33	22	**308**	256	47	156	**10**	**1.66**

A tie between Hubbell and Chuck Klein for MVP. Klein won the Triple Crown: 28 home runs, 120 RBI, .368 batting average. Hubbell gave up six home runs for the whole year.

1934: Dizzy Dean, RHP, St. Louis Cardinals* (NL)

W	L	Pct	GS	CG	IP	H	BB	Ks	ShO	ERA
30	7	**.811**	33	24	311	288	75	195	7	2.66

Definite MVP. Against Paul Waner of the Pittsburgh Pirates, Dizzy easily "slud" right in there.

1936: Carl Hubbell, LHP, New York Giants* (NL)

W	L	Pct	GS	CG	IP	H	BB	Ks	ShO	ERA
26	6	.813	34	25	304	265	57	123	3	**2.31**

Definite MVP. Mel Ott had a good year for the champion Giants. Hubbell, with just 7 HRs, won his last 16 games to start his streak of 24.

1939: Bucky Walters, RHP, Cincinnati Reds* (NL)

W	L	Pct	GS	CG	IP	H	BB	Ks	ShO	ERA
27	11	.711	36	31	319	250	109	137	2	2.29

Probably the true MVP. Walters was a former infielder. The Reds finished first for the first time since 1919.

1942: Mort Cooper, RHP, St. Louis Cardinals* (NL)

W	L	Pct	GS	CG	IP	H	BB	Ks	ShO	ERA
22	7	.759	35	22	297	207	68	152	10	1.78

Definite MVP. Enos "Country" Slaughter of St. Louis placed second. Cooper was the definite winner – no contest.

1943: Spud Chandler, RHP, New York Yankees* (AL)

W	L	Pct	GS	CG	IP	H	BB	Ks	ShO	ERA
20	4	.833	30	20	253	197	54	134	5	1.64

Definite MVP. Luke Appling of the Chicago White Sox had a fine year for a middle infielder. Cannot vote against due to lack of power, but the name of the game is Spud.

1944: Hal Newhouser, LHP, Detroit Tigers* (AL)

W	L	Pct	GS	CG	IP	H	BB	Ks	ShO	ERA
29	9	.763	34	25	312	264	102	**187**	6	2.22

Not the true MVP. World War II military absences included Ted Williams (partial), Luke Appling, Bob Feller, Gene Woodling, Charlie Gehringer, Hank Greenberg, Bill Dickey, Joe Gordon, Phil Rizzuto, Joe DiMaggio, Tommy Henrich, and Joe Collins. Vern Stephens had a good year. Dizzy Trout had a great ERA (2.12) for 352 innings and should have been MVP.

1945: Hal Newhouser, LHP, Detroit Tigers* (AL)

W	L	Pct	GS	CG	IP	H	BB	Ks	ShO	ERA
25	9	.735	**36**	**29**	313	239	110	212	**8**	**1.81**

Definite MVP. Eddie Mayo of the Detroit Tigers was a very poor second. Snuffy Stirnweiss was better than Mayo. Many were still at war. Hal Newhouser was superb.

1950: Jim Konstanty, RHP, Philadelphia Phillies (NL)

W	L	Pct	GS	CG	IP	H	BB	Ks	ERA
16	7	.696	**22**	**74**	152	108	50	56	2.66

Not the true MVP. Del Ennis of the Philadelphia Phillies deserved it for the pennant win (31 home runs, 126 RBI, .311 batting average).

1952: Bobby Shantz, LHP, Philadelphia Athletics (AL)

W	L	Pct	GS	CG	IP	H	BB	Ks	ShO	ERA
24	7	**.774**	33	27	279	230	97	160	5	2.48

Probably the true MVP. Mickey just missed with 87 RBI. Al Rosen and Larry Doby had good years. Shantz had the lowest on-base average in the league, 2.72, and was the Gold Glover.

1956: Don Newcombe, RHP, Brooklyn Dodgers* (NL)

W	L	Pct	GS	CG	IP	H	BB	Ks	ShO	ERA
27	7	**.794**	36	18	268	219	46	139	5	3.06

Hank Aaron (ranked third for MVP) ties with Newcombe. Aaron had 26 home runs and led the league with 200 hits and a .328 batting average.

1963: Sandy Koufax, LHP, Los Angeles Dodgers (NL)

W	L	Pct	GS	CG	IP	H	BB	Ks	ShO	ERA
25	5	.833	40	20	311	214	58	**306**	**11**	**1.88**

Definite MVP. No need to look any further except for Superman! Aaron (third) had an excellent year, better than Dick Groat (second), Willie McCovey, Willie Mays, Vada Pinson, Bill White and Curt Flood. Koufax set the bar at a new all-time height.

1968: Bob Gibson, RHP, St. Louis Cardinals* (NL)

W	L	Pct	GS	CG	IP	H	BB	Ks	ShO	ERA	AVG	OBP
22	9	.710	34	28	304	198	62	**268**	13	**1.12**	.184	.233

1968: Denny McLain, RHP, Detroit Tigers* (AL)

W	L	Pct	GS	CG	IP	H	BB	Ks	ShO	ERA	AVG	OBP
31	6	.838	**41**	**28**	**336**	241	63	280	6	1.96	.200	.233

Both deserved MVP in 1968, the "Year of the Pitcher." Gibson was the true MVP of the two. Pete Rose (second in the National League) had a good year with 210 hits, .335 average, and .394 OBA. Bill Freehan (second in the American League) did not deserve second place. Ken Harrelson and Frank Howard did. Besides, McLain "served up" Mickey's 535 on a platter. Anyone who still doesn't think that a pitcher can be the MVP after seeing Koufax, Gibson, and McClain cannot be a rational fan. The only debate was who was better in 1968.

1971: Vida Blue, LHP, Oakland Athletics (AL)

W	L	Pct	GS	CG	IP	H	BB	Ks	ShO	ERA	AVG	OBP
24	8	.750	39	24	312	209	88	301	**8**	**1.82**	.189	.252

Definite MVP, no contest. Frank Robinson (third) and Brooks Robinson (fourth) did okay.

1981: Rollie Fingers, RHP, Milwaukee Brewers* (AL)

W	L	Pct	SV	IP	H	HR	BB	Ks	ERA
6	3	.667	**28**	78	55	3	13	61	1.04

Definite MVP. Milwaukee could not have possibly won without the brilliant, short-season performance from Rollie Fingers. Rickey Henderson of the Oakland Athletics (second) had a good year.

1984: Willie Hernández, LHP, Detroit Tigers* (AL)

W	L	Pct	G	SV	IP	H	HR	BB	Ks	ERA
9	3	.750	80	32	140	96	6	36	112	1.92

Not the true MVP. Don Mattingly of the New York Yankees was ranked fifth for the MVP award but deserved to win. He was the leader in proficiency and fielding percentage (.996) as well as the Gold Glover. Kent Hrbek (second) of the Minnesota Twins had a good year, but "Donnie Baseball" Mattingly was better.

1986: Roger Clemens, RHP, Boston Red Sox* (AL)

W	L	Pct	GS	CG	IP	H	BB	Ks	ShO	ERA
24	4	.857	33	10	254	179	67	238	1	2.48

Roger Clemens ties with Don Mattingly in my book for 1986 MVP. Clemens delivered 20 games over .500. According to *Total Baseball,* Mattingly delivered at least 57 wins. *Total Baseball* has Don as league leader in proficiency and batting runs over average expectation. Even Pete Rose had no more than 230 hits in a season (680 AB). If Roger Clemens deserved the MVP on the division win, then so did Ron Guidry of the Yankees in 1978!

1992: Dennis Eckersley, RHP, Oakland Athletics (AL)

W	L	Pct	G	SV	IP	H	HR	BB	Ks	ERA
7	1	.875	69	51	80	62	5	11	93	1.91

Definite MVP. Kirby Puckett (second) of the Minnesota Twins had a nice year. No contest.

2011: Justin Verlander, RHP, Detroit Tigers (AL)

W	L	Pct	G	SV	IP	H	HR	BB	Ks	ERA
24	5	.828	34	0	251	174	24	57	250	2.40

Probable MVP. Verlander was up against Jacoby Ellsbury, Jose Bautista, and Miggy Cabrera. Verlander was a narrow winner by Sabermetrics, but Ellsbury and Bautista had league-leading black ink.

2014: Clayton Kershaw, LHP, Los Angeles Dodgers (NL)

W	L	Pct	G	SV	IP	H	HR	BB	Ks	ERA
21	3	.875	27	0	198.1	139	9	31	239	1.77

Definite MVP. Kershaw was the clear winner over Giancarlo Stanton and Andrew McCutchen.

Out of the 25 pitchers listed above, I would say that 13 were the definite MVPs of their respective leagues. Three of those 25 were the probable MVPs, and three tied with their runners-up; all had some serious competition.

The remaining six pitchers, by my estimation, were not the true MVPs. While the MVP award certainly highlights great players, it does not always indicate the player who makes the biggest contributions to his team. In 1999, Pedro Martínez, the truly outstanding pitcher for the Boston Red Sox, proved once again that a pitcher can be the most valuable player of the league. He was so dominant, like no other player in the American League.

Without him, the Red Sox, who lost the pennant to the Yankees by only four games but earned the Wild Card spot for the playoffs, in the toughest division in baseball, would have finished 10 to 15 games back in the pack. But Pedro was not rewarded for his efforts with the MVP. The reason was very obvious: the plethora of players with "outstanding inflated figures." These included Iván Rodríguez, Manny Ramirez, Rafael Palmeiro, Roberto Alomar, Nomar Garciaparra, and a host of others.

Martínez, on the other hand, with a just-above-average Red Sox team, won the Pitching Triple Crown with a 23 – 4 record, 2.07 ERA, and 313 strikeouts. He also set a Major League record of 13.2 strikeouts per 9 innings. The opponents batted only .205 against him, and he let up only nine homers, even with the rabbit ball, low mound, and short fences. The most amazing statistic was the 23 wins for Boston, while pitching in a five-man rotation. In the "real" baseball days of four-man rotations and difficult conditions, he would have won more than 30 games. When it came to the MVP Award, however, he lost out to Iván Rodríguez from the Texas Rangers.

12

"IF YOU DON'T BELIEVE ME, YOU CAN LOOK IT UP!"

"If it wasn't for baseball, I'd be in either the penitentiary or the cemetery." – Babe Ruth

As the late, great sportswriter Red Smith had said, "Baseball is dull only to dull minds." One of the greatest things about baseball is the fact that just when you think that you have seen everything possible, you haven't. Something amazing is just about to come your way.

Casey Stengel, who had 60 years of unique baseball experiences, did his share to astonish fans throughout his playing career. He grew up liking vaudeville and entertainment, which taught him how to play up to a crowd.

Casey took advantage of this talent on May 25, 1918, as on outfielder for the Pittsburgh Pirates. The Pirates were playing against the Dodgers in Ebbets Field. Casey missed a long fly ball and had been booed by the fans. In between innings, Casey visited the Dodgers' bullpen and saw that his former teammate, the Dodgers' Leon Cadore, had caught a sparrow in his glove.

Casey carried the bird back to the Pirates' dugout under his cap and placed it under there again before going to bat. The crowd booed Casey, a former Dodger himself, as he made his way to home plate. Turning to the stands, Casey bowed and lifted his cap. The sparrow flew away, and the audience roared with laughter.

In the first (exhibition) game ever played in Ebbets Field, Casey hit the first home run. While playing for the New York Giants in the 1923 World Series in Game One, Casey hit an inside-the-park home run in Yankee Stadium, in the top of the ninth, to break a 4 – 4 tie. The Yankees went down in order.

Two games later, Casey had another game-winning home run that flew into the right field bleachers. These were the first two World Series homers that were ever hit in Yankee Stadium.

Casey also had a fiery temper and a large will to win. He learned from the master, John McGraw, who learned much from Ned Hanlon, his Hall of Fame manager. Casey's ambition led to some mischievous incidents.

After striking out in a game early in his career, Casey had an umpire tell him, "You're out, big shot." Robert Creamer wrote in *Stengel: His Life and Times*, "The umpire leaned over to get set for the first pitch of the next batter. Casey tiptoed quickly back to the plate and whacked the umpire across the behind with the bat."

Later, both as a player and a manager, Casey was ejected from the game for arguing with the umpires. Can you imagine what would ever happen if he ever committed the despicable crime of spitting on an umpire?

*

Just as amazing as Casey, in his own way, was Ernie Lombardi, the Hall of Fame National League catcher from 1931 to 1947. He primarily caught for the Cincinnati Reds as well as the New York Giants, the Brooklyn Dodgers (Robins), and the Boston Braves. He was a very large, sturdy man of 6'3" and 230 pounds, with big, strong hands. (Seriously, they were huge. One picture of Lombardi shows him holding seven baseballs in one hand. You can look it up!)

But as well-known as he was for his hands, Lombardi was also known for his slow feet. He was so slow that infielders would almost routinely play him back on the edge of the outfield grass, knowing that they could leisurely grab his thunderous hard-hoppers or even routine grounders and still throw him out at first.

Lombardi was a great hitter with a lifetime average of .306. He led the National League in average twice. In 1937, he hit such a ferocious line drive back to Cubs pitcher Larry French that it broke three of French's fingers. (That's almost like facing Satchel Paige three times!) But for all that power, he had unbelievable slowness afoot. Imagine having a lifetime average of .306 with virtually no leg hits. Ernie was, indisputably, slow for a catcher.

When playing for the Giants, Lombardi was noted for hitting 400- foot booming singles off the wall in left. One day, when he was on first and not being held on base by any stretch of the imagination, the pitcher went into his windup! Casey Stengel was coaching first base and yelled to him to go. Lombardi, who had a decent lead, got a great jump and took off. Moments later, he slid into second base and was barely called safe, by a whisker. Lombardi was all smiles as he looked up.

Lombardi also had the incredible experience of catching both of Johnny Vander Meer's back-to-back pseudo no-hitters in 1938. Soon thereafter, the future Hall of Fame pitcher brashly approached Lombardi.

According to one account from late, great slugger Ralph Kiner, Lombardi had a confrontation with Vander Meer not unlike one of Casey's spats with umpires.

There were two kinds of catcher's mitts in Lombardi's era, Kiner explained. "There was a hard one that would *pop* when a good fastball was caught, and there was the very soft one that would make no sound," Kiner said. One day, Vander Meer told Lombardi that he should get one of the gloves that *popped*.

"Lombardi looked at him straight in the eyes and said, 'If you threw the damn ball hard enough, it would pop!'" Kiner said. "Vander Meer was infuriated when Lombardi told him to get back to the mound. He stormed back out there. But Lombardi was also outraged."

Kiner continued, "Vander Meer went into a full windup, reaching back like never before, and let that thing go with all his might. Lombardi merely picked the ball out of the air, bare-handed, and rifled the thing back harder than it had just come in."

Lou Boudreau, Cleveland's Hall of Fame shortstop who later became their manager, wasn't too fast either. Manager Stanley Frank once commented on his slow-moving shortstop, saying, "He is the slowest player since Ernie Lombardi was thrown out at first base trying to stretch a double into a single." Once, however, Lombardi hit four doubles in one game.

*

It takes a very great will to win at baseball. The most determined of players, however, are often mislabeled as something else.

Reggie Jackson has been described as "cocky." Roger Maris and Ted Williams were both called "surly." Bob Gibson was known for being "mean." Carl Yastrzemski was, meanwhile, was referred to as a "prima donna." No true baseball fan, however, can deny the legacies of each player.

It also takes a strong will to pitch even a pseudo no-hitter. Let me tell you about the first "real-pseudo" perfect game.

In 1917, a remarkably talented left-handed starter took the mound for the Boston Red Sox. He had both verve and a tremendous will to win. He was even called "incorrigible" by his biological parents. George Herman "Babe" Ruth was already the best lefty in the league and probably the best pitcher in the league.

On June 23, during the first at bat against the Washington Senators, Ruth got into an argument with umpire Brick Owens. After Ruth thought Owens missed two strikes during the first at bat, as the batter walked, he told Owens to "open [his] god-damned eyes." Owens threatened to have Babe thrown from the game. According to news reports of the time, Babe replied, "You run me out of the game, and I'll bust you in the nose."

Catcher Chester Thomas tried to break up the resulting altercation to no avail. Ruth swung and hit Owens on the back of the neck – ironically, with his right fist instead of his left. It took Red Sox manager Jack Barry and several police officers to escort Ruth from the field.

Babe's replacement, Ernie Shore, pitched the rest of the game. The base runner took off and was thrown out during the next batter's turn and Shore retired the next 26 in-a-row – a "quasi-perfect" game and real no-hitter in the history books.

*

Most baseball fans can recall that Harvey "Hard Luck" Haddix pitched a 12-inning, pseudo-perfect game. This was the greatest game on record ever pitched and then lost on one hit in the 13th inning. What you may not know is that Joe Adcock hit a fair ball over the fence, on the fly, with two men on base, and the final score was 1 – 0!

This game was played in Milwaukee on May 27, 1959. The Braves started the bottom of the 13th inning with Felix Mantilla hitting a very routine grounder to Pirate third baseman Don Hoak. Hoak threw the ball past first baseman Rocky Nelson. With a good throw, Hoak had Mantilla by a mile. There was no question of the error.

Slugger Eddie Mathews was next up and laid down a perfect sacrifice bunt on the first pitch. Hank Aaron was then intentionally walked.

Joe Adcock, who was one of the all-time great "guess hitters," followed in the line-up. He once hit four homers and a double in a nine-inning game. (He should have gone right to Las Vegas!) In the 13th inning, he guessed right and took the first pitch for a ball. Apparently, he guessed at the correct location of the next pitch, too, and hit the ball over the fence near the 394-foot mark in right-center.

The Braves streamed out of their dugout to greet Adcock. The Pirates, led by manager Danny Murtaugh, raced out of the dugout to congratulate their losing pitcher, Haddix, on his most historic feat!

Great emotion and confusion arose, and Hank Aaron did not realize that Adcock's drive had cleared the fence. He merely touched second base and started walking towards the dugout. By the time Aaron's mental error was detected, Adcock was already on third base, and it was too late to turn back. Adcock was already out for passing Aaron, who was also out of the three-foot baseline. In the end, League President Warren Giles ruled that Adcock was credited with only a double, so the final score was officially 1 – 0. Can you imagine if Adcock had passed Aaron and then Aaron drifted out of the baseline, before Mantilla crossed home plate? Are you kidding?

On the other side of the coin was Lou Burdette, the Braves crafty pitcher. He went all 13 innings himself, pitching a shutout. If the game hadn't been bizarre enough, how about the fact that Burdette gave up 12 hits? The only extra base hit in the game was Adcock's over-the- fence double!

Strangely enough, history came close to repeating itself in 1999 during the Mets' crucial drive for the wild card spot. Robin Ventura hit an extra inning, bases loaded, "grand slam single." He drilled the ball over the fence in a tied 3 – 3 game but never touched any bases past first. His teammates and fans poured out on the field and carried him off. The official scorer, the Elias Bureau of Sports, ruled it a single, with a final score of 4 – 3, the Mets over the Braves. Ventura's single was almost as long as one of Lombardi's.

Chris Chambliss of the Yankees was on TV right after, "sweating bullets" because he never got to touch home plate. He had tried, however was blocked by mobbing fans, after hitting an LCS series-ending home run off fireballer Mark Littell of the Kansas City Royals in 1976.

And speaking of peculiar finishes, how about this? In all of recorded baseball history since 1876, there have been only

16 games that ended in the score of 1 – 0, where the only run scored was a steal of home. Out of those 16 games, only one was run had occurred during the ninth inning.

From the *Baseball Research Journal* of the Society for American Baseball Research:

> "April 28, 1906.
>
> "Frank Chance, Cubs vs. Reds at Chicago
>
> "In the last of the ninth in a nothing-nothing game, manager Chance, batting cleanup, took matters into his own hands.
>
> He singled to right off Jake Weimer and moved to second on a one base-blow by Joe Tinker. Johnny Evers strode to the plate, but Chance signaled him back and called on Pat Moran to pinch-hit. Moran rapped a hard one to Jim Delahanty at third, who tried for the double play, and did get Tinker at second, but Joe blocked little Miller Huggins' throw to first. Huggins protested vigorously and demanded that umpire Bill Klem declared Moran out at first because of Tinker's interference. Chance had moved to third on the play and as the quarrel intensified, dashed for home with the game ending run.
>
> "Weimer allowed six hits and Mordecai Brown, the winner, four. There was only one double play: Tinker to Evers to Chance."

A perfect ending.

13

"THE CREAM RISES"

"George [Steinbrenner] thinks that money makes everything right. But money is the root of all evil. It's harder to get a rich man to heaven than it is to get a camel through an eye of a needle, and I didn't make that one up."

— *Reggie Jackson, during his Yankee years*

One of the most pathetic things to see in sports is when an athlete just hangs on too long. Ardent fans remember the great Willie Mays playing for the 1973 New York Mets and hitting a sickly .211. And worse than that was his plate appearance in the World Series, when Mays had all he could do, to *drive* a baseball off home plate, getting a fortuitous scratch single. Great athletes were meant to "go out on top," like Michael Jordan, Wayne Gretzky, John Elway, and Joe DiMaggio.

When baseball was a great game and our true American Pastime, it was a hefty insult for a star to be traded to another team. Great players were icons of one team, period. If Mickey weren't wearing those regal pinstripes, the world wouldn't be in proper order. Actually, Ralph Houk, the Yankees manager, even dared owners to violate this most precious norm of having Mickey in pinstripes when he did not protect Mickey in an expansion draft. He put the ultimate challenge to the other clubs to do the unthinkable: take him in the expansion draft. Besides, Houk finagled an extra quality player through protection.

Babe Ruth was traded before his stellar Yankee career. He made an indelible mark on all of baseball eternity as a Yankee. Ted Williams was on the Red Sox until the end, when he actually smiled as he took his final four-bagger trot around the bases at Fenway Park. The elegant Joe DiMaggio exuded class, going out as a world-champion Yankee in 1949, 1950, and 1951, and called it a career.

Some of the greatest sports heroes in America seemed to need controversy to spur them on to rise above the rest of the field. Joe Namath and Reggie Jackson, in that sense, were cut from the same cloth.

Babe Ruth could carry the weight of the world on his shoulders and enjoyed doing everything in a large manner. "I swing big, with everything I got," Ruth had said. "I hit big or miss big. I like to live as big as I can." That included chowing down seven hot dogs before a game!

Whether Ruth called his shot against Chicago Cubs pitcher Charlie Root in the 1933 World Series is a moot point. Babe was being ruthlessly razed, by the entire bench, throughout the Series and especially that game. He silenced all those bench-jockeying cowboys, however, with one supreme swing.

The Babe always "got up" for the big ones. His psyche went along with his big fulfillment for life. His last great stand came playing for the lowly Boston Braves, as a haggard 41-year-old man. Playing one of his last games in Pittsburgh in a very spacious Forbes Field, Ruth hit three home runs, including his hardest-hit home run ever.

For the last two, Ruth faced Guy Bush, his old rival from the Cubs. In the seventh inning, Ruth hit home run number 714. "I never saw a ball hit so hard before or since," Bush later commented. "It was unbelievably long, completely over the roof of the park! Nobody had ever hit the ball out of the park before. It traveled 600 feet."

Actually, two men have done this since. Ted Beard, the strapping Pirates outfielder, matched the feat. So did the incomparable Mickey Mantle in an exhibition game just before he connected off pitcher Chuck Stobbs in Washington. Many fans mistakenly think that the shot of Stobbs was Mickey's longest shot.

Babe played a couple more games and hurt his knee, and that was that. He made his last great statement. How many players have ever hit three homers in a game in their prime? How many finished with this majesty?

This last hurrah was truly grandiose. It characterized the Babe, the "Sultan of Swat," at his best and how he should always be remembered. This accentuated his God-given talent and dwarfed all the other players of that era. Not even Jimmy "Double X" Foxx, Lou Gehrig, or Hank Greenberg could match the crowning end for the "King of the Game." Ted Williams, the "Splendid Splinter," finally came to the last game of his most illustrious career. He had become the game's greatest "pure hitter." He defied the shift and the press, just as he had defied the enemy in the Korean War so many times. (He flew 39 combat missions.)

In his prime, Ted refused to lose and played hard until the end. Going into the last day of 1941, his batting average was .39955. Officially, that was a clean .400. The Red Sox had not just one game to play that day, but two. Ted demanded that he play in both, or else he wasn't worthy of .400! Ken Griffey, Sr., once came out early on the last day of the season, thinking that he had a lock on the batting title, only to lose out to Bill Madlock. "Teddy Boy" was different. He promptly went 6 – 8 and finished with a cool .4057, which is an official .406. Nobody has done this since. Williams was the first to hit the coveted mark of .400 since Harry Heilmann in the AL, in 1923, and the fabulous Bill Terry in the NL, in 1930.

The stage was set for Ted's last game. It was September of 1960. He came up to at bat for the last time forever. The very bitter, biting wind cut through the right-field stands and swirled in towards home plate. The sky was ominous gray. Ted was older now and could just hit in the high .300's! "Teddy Boy" waved his magic wand at the last ball he ever hit. He defied his age, gravity, and all other odds. The ball sailed into the stands. Rounding all the bases, Ted even smiled, as opposed to once getting fined $5,000 for spitting at fans.

But the most astounding feat, even greater than hitting in 56 straight games, was what Joe D., "The Yankee Clipper," did in 1949. DiMaggio had more self-pride and Yankee pride than anyone who ever wore the majestic pinstripes. In the 1949 season, he was also fighting an agonizing bone spur on his right heel.

Joe DiMaggio, more than any other Yankee, understood the rivalry between his team and the Boston Red Sox. His own brother had played for the enemy. Baseball is the personification of life, and this competition was a civil war: brother vs. brother, American vs. American, one big winner and one big loser. To this day, there are no other rivalries that match up on the same emotional plane. Many Madison Avenue boys have tried to fabricate one of this magnitude. But these are the *real* Hatfields and McCoys. On June 28, 1949, rookie New York Yankees manager Casey Stengel stalled before handing in his lineup card. Soon, DiMaggio nodded affirmatively, and then they were both ready. Joe had not played in all of spring training and had missed the entire first 65 games of the season. But this was different; it was against Boston and at Fenway Park. Up to that point, the league games had felt like practice. Baseball *really* started that night, with the crowd practically overflowing into the park.

DiMaggio came to bat in the second inning. After a few foul balls, he finally hit a single over the shortstop's head. In the third, the Yankees had a 3 – 0 lead when DiMaggio got up and hit a two-run homer. The Red Sox came back with four runs. DiMaggio's homer supplied the margin of victory.

The next afternoon, the Red Sox shot ahead 7 – 1 going into the fifth. DiMaggio came up with two outs and two men on base and hit a three-run homer. Woodling doubled home three more in the seventh to tie the game. In the eighth inning, DiMaggio hit another homer, making it 8 – 7. The Yankees won 9 – 7.

The last game of the three-game set saw the Red Sox score first again. The Yankees tied it 1 – 1 in the third inning and made it 3 – 1 in the fourth. The Red Sox scored a run in the fifth to close the gap to 3 – 2, and the score stayed that way until the seventh. Then, with two men on, DiMaggio swung at a 3 – 2 pitch and hit another homer, a tremendous poke off the light tower above the left-field wall, to break the game open 6 – 2. The Yankees won 6 – 3.

It was absolutely a remarkable performance. DiMaggio hit four home runs, batted in 9 runs, caught 13 balls in the outfield, and lifted the Yankees' spirits immeasurably. And it wasn't over yet.

The 1949 season went on until just two games remained. The Red Sox held a one-game lead over the Yankees. They were to play each other at the "House that Ruth Built" for all the marbles. DiMaggio had been out of the lineup with a terrible flu; he had just lost 10 pounds. When Joe returned to center stage, majestic Yankee Stadium, the drama was about to unfold.

DiMaggio single-handedly tied the game, bringing the score to 4 – 4 by the fifth inning. But he was so sick, he had to come out of the game. Johnny Lindell hit the game-winning home run for the Yankees afterwards. The next day, October 2, 1949, was the final showdown for the pennant. DiMaggio played, but had to leave the game early once more. Yet if it hadn't been for his grit, the Yankees wouldn't have won the pennant or the World Series that season.

Joe DiMaggio went out on top with class, like Ruth and Williams. He won a World Series championship each year from 1949 through 1951 and then "hung up his spikes." Some were surprised years later as this very private man agreed to represent Mr. Coffee. He did drink an excessive amount during his playing days. I'm not sure, but I wouldn't be surprised if he took it with cream.

14

OTHER NEAT BASEBALL EXPRESSIONS

In the old Detroit stadium, the sign above the entrance to the visitors' clubhouse read:
    "Visitors' Clubhouse: No Visitors Allowed."

In 1976, arbitrator Peter Seitz rocked the world. He ruled that Andy Messersmith and Dave McNally were *real* free agents. They were not, he said, *pseudo* free agents like Catfish Hunter, whom Oakland A's owner Charles O. Finley had declared a free agent due to a breach of contract. Messersmith and McNally, and all who followed, were able to negotiate a contract with any baseball organization that they chose. With the stroke of the mighty pen, we passed through a 100-year-old time warp and began the era of free agency.

"Free agents" – what an oxymoron. It makes more sense to say that Joe DiMaggio "reeked of class." And the plain *morons* were the owners who got caught up in the ludicrous bidding wars. But the biggest losers for all eternity are the *real* baseball fans and baseball itself.

Statistical analysts could now have a field day with the relative values of those players to determine if they were worth the price. Worth, in a purely economic sense, could be defined as a player who drew enough additional fans into each game that he played to offset his own salary increase. Early in this new era, Catfish Hunter came close to doing exactly that. With the nonsensical salaries of today, the stadiums would have to be so expansive that the outfield fence would have to neatly merge with the Great Wall of China...and players would still only hit 330-foot homers.

If these high-paid players could win the World Series for their teams, one could also argue that the astronomical salaries are worth the investment. Few, however, have been successful. In the beginning, only Catfish Hunter, Reggie Jackson, Goose Gossage, and Pete Rose led their teams to victory.

Evidently, the late Wayne Huizenga, the original owner of the Florida Marlins, would not have agreed with this definition of worth. After winning the world championship, he sold off his players like pawns. There was no real commissioner to stop him, like the time that Charles Finley traded away star pitchers Vida Blue, Rollie Fingers, and the very talented and underrated Joe Rudi. Bowie Kuhn, the commissioner, nullified the trade, to keep the balance of the league and for the overall "good of the game."

Here we are speaking of the *business of baseball*. The money is green, but the fields aren't even real anymore.

The real "Hit and Run" Award (also known as the "Cleaners" Award, as in, "I took them to the cleaners") belongs to pitcher Wayne Garland. A very close second would be Hideki Irabu, who should have earned the "Yo-yo Award," in 1976. Let's not forget Baltimore's Joey Albert Belle, whose bum hip cost Baltimore a cool $37 million!

Wayne Garland was 20 – 7 for the Baltimore Orioles and then became a free agent. We know that pitching is 90 percent of the game, and Cleveland signed him for $2.15 million over 10 years. That doesn't seem like much today, as the average salary is many millions of dollars. But in 1976, the average MLB salary was $52,300 and never in history was a 10-year contract given.

Garland lost 19 games the first year for the Indians and blew his arm out by the second year. For his millions, he went 28 – 48. He truly felt terrible about this, but there was nothing he could do; he couldn't hit. The point is that statistics cannot, never could, and never will be able to predict the future of baseball. Our great statistical analysts can only brilliantly talk about the past. In terms of watching *poor* Wayne Garland struggle, I would much rather watch Roger Craig of the New York Mets lose 24 and 22 games.

However, Garland wasn't the only bust. Don Gullett, the one-time ace of Cincinnati, won 14 games for the Yankees in 1977 and blew out his arm in 1978. Two years into his six-year contract, he was finished. Campy Campaneris got a five-year contract with Texas at the age of 34 and lasted only two of them. Gene Tenace, the Oakland catcher whose clutch homers produced big in the World series victories for the A's, was signed by Ray Kroc. Kroc was the outspoken owner of the Padres and fast food franchise McDonald's. Tenace signed for $1.8 million over five years, finishing when he was 36 years old. That was still a lot of hamburgers. In 1999, Angels pitcher Tim Belcher sat out the last two weeks with a sore shoulder. Belcher finished with a record of 6 – 8, 6.73 ERA, in the first of a two-year, $10 million "free agent" contract!

The infancy of free agency brought these players good

fortune, as Marvin Miller had predicted. Perhaps luck plays a role in these deals, too.

For some players, it's more like beginner's luck. In 1952, Hoyt Wilhelm of the Orioles came to the plate for the first time in his career and proceeded to hit a home run. I hope that he wasn't holding his breath for his next one because after playing 1,070 games as a future Hall of Fame pitcher, it never happened again.

More amazing was pitcher Bobo Holloman, who pitched a pseudo no-hitter for the old St. Louis Browns in 1953. It was his first assignment ever. He was also out of baseball within one year. In 1891 and 1892, two other pitchers had the same incredible feat, but managed to stay in the game.

How about the "Luckiest Pitcher Alive" Award? Nine players of the 1946 Spokane Indians Class B Western International League team were killed when their bus went off a mountain on its way from Oregon to Washington. Future major leaguer Jack Lohrke had gotten off at the last stop, with orders to report to San Diego, and was ever known as "Lucky."

Hard-luck pitchers are typically labeled as pitchers who pitch quite well, but their teams don't score many runs for them. Harvey Haddix is arguably the hardest-luck pitcher in history, on a one-time stint, as we have discussed. Pedro Martinez once pitched nine perfect innings as a member of the Montreal Expos only to lose his bid in the 10th inning against the San Diego Padres.

There have been others who have gone nine hitless innings and then have lost the game in extra innings, too. Bobo Newsome of the St. Louis Browns was one. Others were Cleveland's Earl Moore, Leon "Red" Ames of the Giants, the Yankees' Tom Hughes in 1910, Brooklyn's Harry McIntire (10 innings, 0 hits), Chicago's Jim Scott, Ken Johnson of the

Astros, Andy Hawkins of the Yankees, and Jim Maloney of the Cincinnati Reds with his incredulous pitching line. Maloney pitched a 10-inning pseudo no-hitter and lost in the 11th on June 14, 1965. Then he pitched another 10-inning pseudo no-hitter on August 19 and managed to win. Nolan Ryan and "Lefty" Steve Carlton once struck out 19 batters in a game and lost.

Conversely, Oakland pitchers Johnny "Blue Moon" Odom and Francisco Barrios, who pitched a pseudo no-hitter while walking eleven batters, may exemplify good-luck pitchers. Joe Crowley, the Chicago White Sox hurler, pitched a "monsterpiece" as he walked seven during his 1986 pseudo no-hitter. Believe it or not, he never won another game in his Major League career! Mitch "Wild Thing" Williams, who came in as a reliever for the Phillies, never pitched one pitch and earned a win. He picked a runner off base. A similar situation happened again in 1998.

The platoon system, as many know it, plays a man for gaining a righty-lefty or vice versa advantage in the lineup. Most think that Yankees manager Casey Stengel started this when he would often platoon Hank Bauer for Gene Woodling. Casey was a big proponent of this method, but it was started years earlier *because of Casey* and other players of his era.

In 1912 with the Brooklyn Dodgers, Casey hit a decent .316. His manager Bill Dahlen noticed that Casey, who was left-handed, hit .351 off of right-handed pitchers and only .251 off of lefties. "The seeds of his own time, platooning at bat," Creamer said in *Stengel: His Life and Times,* "were already planted."

Many players were good in the clutch. Yankees fans all know about Babe, Lou, Whitey, Yogi, Joe D., Hank Bauer, Bobby Richardson, Billy Martin, and Mickey, but how about

Casey Stengel as a World Series player? He hit .393. Likewise, Christy Mathewson, the New York Giants ace, had a World Series lifetime ERA of 11 games averaging 1.06, which is only second to Sandy Koufax's eight games with a miniscule ERA of 0.95, with a *real* strike zone.

Today, the "strike zone" is absolutely ridiculous. The true strike zone should be that from the armpits to the knees and over the plate. On the other side of the coin, there is a whole generation of players who can only "hit their pitch." That shows how inept they are or that they just swing for the fences too much, and worry about their huge contracts, which are built statistics. The best "bad ball hitters" who ever played were Yogi Berra, Hank Aaron, Ducky Medwick of the St. Louis "Gas House Gang," Roberto Clemente, and Vladimir Guerrero. All are Hall of Famers because they could play *real baseball*.

In one crucial game, the opposing pitcher wanted nothing to do with Yogi Berra. Late in the game, with men on base, Yogi was too big of a threat. Instead of intentionally walking Yogi, the pitcher threw one that was very low and a foot outside. Yogi golfed into the left-field bleachers and turned the game around.

As Yogi was rounding third, the pitcher was yelling, "That was a terrible pitch! That was a terrible pitch!" Yogi, (according to Allen Barra in his book *Yogi Berra)*, had replied, "Looked good to me!"

Casey Stengel, according to Robert Creamer, had his own distinctive way of communicating on and off the diamond – "Stengelese," if you will. At each home plate meeting, he tells the umpires, "Let's commence this thing." When the game started, he would often play inside ball and encourage his men to "Butcher Boy" the ball and hit the '01 "Baltimore Chop."

When someone unknowingly asked Casey about a person who was deceased, Casey replied with, "At the present time, he is dead."

About Mantle, Casey once said, "The kid runs so fast he doesn't even bend the grass when he steps on it." He also said, upon seeing Mantle, in his first spring training, "My God, the kid runs faster than Cobb."

Mickey wasn't the only subject of Casey's unique expressions. When Casey would see the great Satchel Paige warming up in the Indians bullpen, he would implore his men to, "Get runs now before Father Time comes in!"

According to legend, the "bullpen" got its name from the Bull Durham tobacco signs near where the relievers warmed up. My theory is different. It may have originated when visiting right fielders would often reside, for a half of an inning, in the right-field area of Ebbets Field. The conversations must have been quite *interesting*. Sometimes, Casey would stop in and lay it on. Just imagine the comments that were made when Casey returned to play center field! Maybe that's where his "Stengelese" originated. When he left, undoubtedly the opponents would say, "What bull!"

And how can we end this chapter without Dizzy Dean? He would often announce that the player just "slud" in there. When pitching, he used to call a lazy high pop-up to the outfield a "tall can of corn." Most likely, as a farm boy, the arc reminded him of the way corn grew.

One day, when Dizzy was pitching, he was clocked on the head with a line drive. He was taken to the hospital for X-rays. Apparently, he was okay. The next morning's headlines read: "X-rays of Dizzy Dean's Head Show Nothing."

15

"REAL" HALL OF FAMERS

It's unthinkable that "Slats" is not in the Hall of Fame. The only ones who were better at shortstop were Honus Wagner and The Wizard of Oz.

This chapter contains facts, vital information, and opinions about some truly great ball players. Every one of these players should be in the Baseball Hall of Fame. *This is not a statistically based chapter.* If statistics alone are your criteria for evaluating great ball players, please skip this discussion.

Outfield:

"Shoeless" Joe Jackson
The largest factor one could mention to Jackson's credit was not his .356 lifetime average. It was the fact that Babe Ruth modeled his swing after Joe Jackson because "He was the best there was." Jackson was terrific in the dead ball era. After the "Black Sox" scandal of 1919, Jackson was acquitted by a court of law and banished for life by the league's power-hungry,

iron-fisted first commissioner, Judge Kenesaw Mountain Landis, *for the good of the game!* This vote is a "shoe-in."

Pete "Charley Hustle" Rose
Some of my baseball friends will take exception with this. I do think that Rose belongs in Cooperstown, but with the convincing evidence of the Dowd report, he should not be let back on the field until he is cleared by the Commissioner and a court of law or redeems himself with the public. If you don't have an open mind about Rose, then consider throwing Ty Cobb and others out of the Hall. If you do eliminate a few, please save room for Jim Kaat, Tommy John, and Tony Oliva.

Roger Maris

I still consider Roger as the real Home Run King for a season. If you think that Roger was a "One-Year Wonder," please don't even read another page of this book. We will never be on the same page.

First of all, Roger Maris made for a winning team in a very large way. A winning cohesiveness is the most vital and most valuable intangible that one can achieve in the game. When Mickey or Joe D. walked on the field, for instance, they made everyone play up to their potential. Wherever Roger Maris played, the rest of the players "played up" due to his positive influence. That is what a team sport is all about. It is not about personal records and $300 million contracts. No one person can carry the entire load in a team sport.

Next, Roger was a great fielder with excellent range and a "gun- like" arm. He was as good as the great Al Kaline, but with more power. Roger had the knack for *always* throwing to the right base, which personified his keen baseball sense. Roger was the American League MVP in both 1960 and 1961. In 1962, Roger tore a ligament in his thumb and the Yankees owners would not let him sit out; they were too hungry for the "bank." Without being able to grip the bat, Roger still hit 33! Then he made for a winning team in St. Louis. He was a great clutch hitter.

Maris was a big, strong football player as a youth as an All-State halfback in North Dakota. Maris was an exceptionally good runner on the base paths, too. He could break up the double play like very few others had ever done. (Mickey, however, was the best at this.) Roger didn't hesitate to plow someone over when it made sense or was critical for a team win.

For all those who have forgotten, Roger owned the most precious record in baseball and held it longer than Babe Ruth. The worst thing about the new home run record is that most people will forget how great of an all-around team ball player Roger was and what a fine gentleman he was, too.

First Base:

Don Mattingly

Don Mattingly was the Captain and the glue of the Yankees. He was an excellent hitter for average, very good for production and great in the clutch. Mattingly was also the best fielding first basemen of his generation and truly the team leader. He was a more dominant force than Dave Winfield, until his back deteriorated. Winfield deservedly made the Hall of Fame. Mattingly and Winfield had parallel careers in a sense that they both warmed up, had their prime streak, injured their backs, and finished out their careers.

Mattingly was better in his streak than Winfield was in his. David, however, played for 22 years compared to Mattingly's 13, and he amassed outstanding numbers. Don's dominant streak of excellence lasted six years, from 1984 to 1989. David's streak of excellence lasted seven years from 1982 to 1989. In Don's streak, he averaged 204 hits a year, far surpassing Dave's average of 168 hits each season. Mattingly averaged more doubles and the same number of home runs per year. He also surpassed Winfield in average, slugging percentage, RBIs, and league-leading statistics (11 – 1), not to mention his grand slam record. Don won nine Gold Glove Awards and hit much better in postseason play (over .400).

So, what's your rap on Mattingly? That he only played for 13 years?

Gil Hodges

Gil Hodges was an All-Star player who was an integral part of the fabulous Brooklyn Dodger Teams in the late 1940s through the 1950s, until they moved in 1958. He was also the heady manager who led the Mets to their astounding 1969 pennant and World Series Championship. He made for a winning team at bat, on the field, and in the clubhouse.

Hodges was overshadowed by Duke Snider. For more than a decade, Gil led all first basemen in home runs and hit more homers in the 1950s except Duke Snider. In the field, he was a stellar first sacker. He was a Gold Glove-caliber fielder for nearly every year of his career.

In the clubhouse, Hodges was a steady, driving influence, so much so that he was named a manager of the Washington Senators after his playing days. He actually improved the hapless Senators -- what a miracle! His next miracle came in 1969 with the Mets and their defeat of the mighty Baltimore Orioles, which was an astounding feat!

Gil's stats are outstanding for his era, for those who depend on that. It's a shame that he did not make the Hall of Fame before he passed away, like Ron Santo, too.

Shortstop:

Marty "Slats" Marion

Out of all of my selections, Marty Marion should be in the Hall of Fame before anybody else! He was the preeminent shortstop of the 1940s for the Cardinals. He was the glue that held the team together. Without the flips, he was the Ozzie Smith of his decade. (Smith, the remarkable agile and acrobatic shortstop for the Cardinals, was the standout of his era.)

Marty Marion was the team leader of the World Series champion Cardinals, just as Phil Rizzuto was for the Yankees. Phil, Marty, and Harold "Pee Wee" Reese were the spark plugs who led their teams to numerous championships in their league, some being the World Series. Reese, leading off for the Dodgers, won one World Series Championship and played in seven. Both Rizzuto and Reese have been enshrined in the Hall of Fame.

Eyewitnesses will also admit that Marion was a touch better in the field than Rizzuto, whom Casey thought was even better than the great Honus Wagner was. Granted, Marion may not have been quite as good as Honus Wagner, but nobody who ever played was. Arky Vaughan was probably his only other superior besides Hans.

"Slats" was an All-Star for eight of the 12 years he played. Marion played in four World Series, winning three. He had his own long, lean, superb fielding style. He led the league in fielding 25 percent of the time, which was better than Hall of Famer "Rabbit" Maranville. But please remember that this statistic is *not* indicative of his fielding greatness.

Marion was the catalyst of the Cardinal team that beat Joe McCarthy's 1942 Yankees for McCarthy's only World Series loss. He was the National League's MVP in 1944. Marty Marion had a higher lifetime average, on base percentage and slugging percentage, than Maranville and Luis Aparicio. He is truly in the elite class of shortstops, which is a cut above all others.

Grantland Rice, the world's best sports columnist of old, called Marion "one of the game's finest fielders." *What is the Veterans Committee waiting for?*

Catcher:

Thurman Munson

Munson was great. Throw out all your statistics now. He *did* have excellent numbers in his career as the Rookie of the Year, a seven-time All-Star, and the 1976 American League MVP. He had a nearly .300 lifetime average as a catcher and three Gold Gloves Awards in a row, and he was definitely better than 2000 Hall of Famer Carlton Fisk.

But those statistics are not Munson's only credentials. Munson was the best ball player of his era on a psychological level. He was a better and more feared clutch performer with the game on the line than the great Pete Rose or Reggie Jackson. This intensity meant throwing out a key runner to foil a rally or coming up big at the plate. He emulated Yankee Pride in the footsteps of Ruth, Gehrig, Joe D., Yogi and Mickey. He was a great Captain and as quick as there ever was on a bunt, like the great Bill Dickey. It was nearly impossible to bunt between him and Ron Guidry. He could unconventionally throw runners out from any angle on sure will and determination, mandated by how critical the play was to winning. He handled the pitching staff in a supreme fashion, just as he handled Reggie's malarkey.

Munson was a great clutch hitter in postseason play, too. He hit in 16 straight postseason games. His League Championship Series .339 and World Series .373 were some of the finest batting averages of all time. With this, the Captain taught the Yankees how to perform under pressure and how to win at the World Series-level of play. Watching Munson work with Catfish Hunter was a *real* slice of baseball euphoria. Munson was the best of his era and could compete with anyone in baseball history, including Johnny Bench. He would rise to the occasion and win.

Pitcher:

Ron "Louisiana Lightning" Guidry
What Guidry did has really gone unnoticed. His win-loss record is comparable to the great Sandy Koufax! Guidry had a lifetime winning percentage of .651; for his nine prime years, he held an astounding .694.

But that is hardly the whole story. Ron Guidry single-handedly held the Yankees team and staff together like no other pitcher in history. In the great comeback season of 1978, when the Yankees were behind by 14 games in August, Guidry kept the Yankees in the pennant race by winning his first 13 games. He put a stop to 14 losing streaks, which taught his team how to fight. That is more valuable than his all-time best winning percentage ever for a season of .893, while going 25 – 3!

Guidry was also, far and away, the best fielding pitcher of his time. Atlanta's four-time Cy Young winner and Hall of Famer Greg Maddux was a great fielder on ground balls. Nobody ever played the bunt better than "Louisiana Lightning." That is the way the game should be played, but few players do. He often led the league in wins, winning percentage, shutouts, complete games, ERA, and fielding. He won the big games, including the great playoff game against the Red Sox in 1978, and earned five Gold Gloves in a row. Remembering that they have the ridiculous DH rule in the American League, what more can a guy do?

Player	G	IP	W	L	Pct	SO	BB	ERA
Koufax	397	2324	165	87	.655	2396	817	2.76
Guidry	368	2392	170	91	.651	1778	633	3.29
Drysdale	518	3432	209	166	.557	2486	855	2.95

If Ron "Gator" Guidry pitched as much as Don Drysdale, he would have won 239 games and lost only 127. He has much more "black ink" (league-leading statistics) than Drysdale. Guidry's record for percentage of wins is like the great Whitey Ford's.

16

A CLUTCH PERFORMER

"Nobody loved the game of baseball more than Gary Carter. Nobody enjoyed playing the game of baseball more than Gary Carter. He wore his heart on his sleeve every inning he played. For a catcher to play with that intensity in every game is special."
– *Tom Seaver, Hall of Fame Pitcher*

Imagine a seven-year-old entering the *Pass, Punt, and Kick* competition. A typical child his age might have some anxiety about it. This kid, however, was uniquely cool. He won his local and regional competitions and went on to the national finals. For him, the *larger* the crowd, the *better* he seemed to perform. He had already beaten everyone in his age bracket (and then some) to capture the national title.

This particular kid was very clean cut and confident in his skills, without being cocky. He was willing to pay the price of hard work and conditioning, keeping his body at peak performance levels, without ever using drugs, to prepare for his competition.

He passed up more than 100 football scholarships to fulfill a dream of playing major league baseball. During his Triple-A stint with the Memphis Blues, he came close to winning an International League championship. In one game, in the best-out-of-five series, he ripped two home runs and drove in six runs. The next day's headline read, "Carter 6 – Rochester Red Wings 4." His team then lost the series at home.

The kid hated to lose. He lived by Vince Lombardi's famed statement, "Show me a good loser, and I'll show you a loser." (But he was also a genuine real "nice guy," Leo.)

That kid was Gary Carter. For the first decade of his career, Gary played in an obscure Major League city and a very difficult park in Montreal, in front of sparse crowds. By 1981, he played in front of a huge All-Star crowd in Cleveland. He hit two home runs and won the Arch Ward Trophy for being named MVP. Only the great Ted Williams, Arky Vaughan, Willie McCovey, and Al Rosen had ever done that. In 1981, Gary Carter also played in front of some large crowds against the Phillies and Dodgers in postseason play and hit .421 and .438. Carter was again the All-Star MVP in 1984.

In 1985, Gary "Kid 8" Carter got traded to the New York Mets, and that was just what he needed. He was stuck in Montreal with the great Andre "The Hawk" Dawson and the future Hall of Famer Tim Raines. Now he was *forced* to play in front of a huge crowd and under the intense scrutiny of the New York City press. So many, like New York Yankees pitcher Ed Whitson, were clearly unsuccessful in this venue.

The Mets were already drawing three million fans a year, long before the baseball strike and after the era of "Tom Terrific" Seaver. Surprisingly to New York and unnoticed in Montreal, Gary Carter was also terrific. He had already led the league in fielding percentage twice, and in 1978, he set a Major League record of having only one passed ball in 157 games. Remember that the "splitter" was already in vogue, and often the ball wouldn't be on the ground but sailing like mad through the air. Carter was named the Co-Captain of the Mets in 1988, joining Keith Hernandez, who was named in 1987.

So how good were Carter's skills? In 1984, while playing for Montreal, his manager Bill Virdon started him at first base 25 times to save on his wear and tear a bit, in front of Pete Rose. Carter said that, "Virdon, who was a very slick center fielder and had a keen eye for talent, always put in our best defensive players regardless of personality." In 1984, Carter led the National League in RBIs, and Montreal traded him! He was clearly the National League's best catcher – Hall of Fame caliber – since Johnny Bench.

In 1986, Gary finally got to play for another national title. This time, it was the coveted World Series crown against the Boston Red Sox. In Game Six, with Boston leading the Series 3 – 2, the game went into the 10th inning. The Red Sox had just scored two runs in the top of the inning to take a 5 – 3 lead. The Red Sox were trying to do the impossible! They were just one little out from breaking the "Curse of the Bambino." But the 100-year-sentence wasn't up yet.

Boston manager John McNamara usually sent in Dave Stapleton for defensive purposes, for the now gimpy-ankled Bill Buckner. Buckner had an outstanding career in the National League. He had primarily played for the Cubs, who won about as many times as the Washington Senators. Carter told me that, "He wanted to have Billy Buckner on the field, finally as a World Series winner." Was this the ultimate twist of ironic fate or what? This, undoubtedly, was a decision of fate!

. Ecstatic anticipation was in the air. History was about to be completed. Finally, after a curse of many generations of futility and frustration, the Boston Red Sox would finally, after eons, win another World Series! The champagne was just thrown on ice in the Red Sox locker room. The reporters scurried around, setting up their cameras and microphones in the Red Sox locker room. The World Series trophy was moved over for the presentation to the Red Sox.

In the Mets locker room, Kevin Mitchell, who was not playing, had already taken off his clothes, all of them. Why hassle with "the agony of defeat" in the face of reporters? There were now two outs, and nobody was even on base.

This time, the whole world was watching, and the enthusiastic and overflowing Shea Stadium crowd was clinging to hope. "Kid" Carter was next up. He reached inside of himself and prayed for strength. He didn't want to be the answer to a 1986 trivia question. It had been 12 years since that defeat in front of the hometown crowd at Memphis, Tennessee. But the feeling of losing never quite leaves. With a 2-1 count, his prayers were answered. He hit a single into left field off the reliever for Roger Clemens, Calvin Schiraldi and ignited the spark.

Davey Johnson then called on Kevin Mitchell to pinch hit. (He did, thankfully, put his clothes back on first.) Mitchell also hit a single to left. Carter wisely stopped at second base, playing "station to station," for the time being. He knew that this was not any time to stray and get picked off.

Next up was Ray Knight. Ironically, Bill Fischer, who delivered the pitch that Mickey drove off the top of the very facade of Yankee Stadium, was the Red Sox pitching coach! He made a visit to the mound. Schiraldi got two quick strikes on Knight. But then Knight fisted a "broken-bat" single to center.

Gary Carter changed his mind set and said, "I've got to

score. I got up on my toes and raced home and incited my team," as he stormed into the dugout. Mitchell raced to third.

Closer Bob Stanley relieved Schiraldi, and Mookie Wilson stepped into the batter's box. Mookie swung and missed for 0 – 1, followed by ball, ball, foul ball, foul ball again, foul ball again, and then Stanley uncorked a wild pitch! The TV announcers had just anointed him with "the kiss of death," as they claimed how few wild pitches Stanley had thrown all year!

At that point, I told my seven-year-old son Adam that Stanley was going to throw a wild pitch.

He said, "How do you know?"

I just said, "Watch," based on the "the kiss of death," a corollary of a "play of fate."

Stanley threw a wild pitch, and Kevin Mitchell scampered home to tie the game. The "Big Apple" was salivating at the mouth. Knight raced to second base.

Stanley composed himself on a 3 – 2 pitch, and Mookie fouled off two more pitches. Mookie then hit a twisting ball of fate that stayed just fair, inside the first base line. Buckner was playing very deep (20-plus feet behind the bag, guarding the line), and for a split second, as the ball gyrated towards him, he looked up at Stanley to see if he would be covering first base. An instant later, Billy Buckner became eternal friends with Ralph Branca, Ralph Terry, and Mickey Owens.

Although the Red Sox were leading in the next game, Game Seven, the ending was already a foregone conclusion. The whole world knew the Red Sox would lose because it was just playing out fate's scenario.

In 1978 during the playoff "Bucky Dent" game, my wife asked, "How are we doing?"

When I reported that it was 2 – 0, she cringed. I said, "Don't worry, it will happen."

So, what compelled a kid like Carter to rise to the occasion? Is it learned or innate? Is a winner a winner and a born loser always a loser?

At just 12 years old, Gary found out just how precious life is. His mother was diagnosed with leukemia. He was protected from this fact, as that was the thinking in the 1950s and '60s of how to handle medical tragedies with children. She passed away just six months later.

Gary knew that he loved baseball and had excellent athletic abilities well before the *Pass, Punt, and Kick* competition. He had a great work ethic throughout his entire career. He took care of his body and his God-given talent to the best of his ability. But he also learned that time is so precious that you must play to the fullest and lives in appreciation each and every day. Those fortunate people who never "walked a mile in another person's shoes" certainly cannot appreciate that energy. The learned pace of a person with a life experience as such often gets misinterpreted as being brash or cocky. But who cares how naïve people try to label it?

So, what "Kid" Carter brought to the Mets and the "Big Apple," the showcase of the world, was exactly the same winning psychology that Munson, Hunter, and Jackson brought to the Yankees and Rose brought to the Phillies. Carter was the ultimate team player.

Gary told me that his greatest thrill in sports was winning the Seventh Game of the 1986 World Series and being on the field with the Mets, admiring all of them. Together, they celebrated the ultimate team victory. He wore his 1986 World Series Championship ring with pride.

Confident and driven for success because of the fragileness of life – that was who Gary Carter was. He was a true leader who performed best under pressure and had the unique ability to uphold this terrific level of play, in front of enormous crowds, ever since the age of seven.

Gary Carter was a wonderful family man with three children. For a while, he stayed busy broadcasting in the Florida Marlins organization. Quite possibly, there was a connection between the incredible catcher Charles Johnson and future Hall of Famer Gary Carter. Carter also announced for the Expos as Johnson brought his "tools of ignorance" to the Orioles.

The "Kid" also stepped up to the plate for the National Leukemia Foundation by raising more than $1 million. He spoke and inspired others about life at banquettes and stayed busy by giving back to mankind.

Gary Carter was rightfully voted into the Baseball Hall of Fame at Cooperstown, New York, in 2003. He had exceptional skills, ethics, and drive and delivered in the clutch, over and over, like Yogi. He won with a lesser team than Bench and had the leadership character of Munson. He also, most certainly, belongs in the "Hall of Fame of Life" on the first ballot.

17

"GOOD ON PAPER"

Once, a know-it-all reporter had the nerve to challenge the great Joe DiMaggio on his fielding abilities. The stupid kid asked, "Joe, if you're such a great fielder, why is it that you don't lead the league in fielding percentage?"

Joe remarked, "I make errors on balls that other players don't even get close to!"

Joe never let that reporter into the clubhouse again.

As a dyed-in-the-wool New York Yankees fan, I scrutinized every move that George Steinbrenner made after he had become the principal owner in 1973. At first, I was not sure that George had a real trained eye for talent, or else he had the wrong advice. He should have had *real* scouts and general managers versus political appointments or whatever.

Many others didn't like Mr. Steinbrenner, either. But you must preface all discussions about George on two facts.

First is the fact that, shortly after George came into power, the rules of the *business of baseball* had changed more with a single stroke of Peter Seitz's pen than in 100-plus years of baseball existence. Steinbrenner did not make up these rules. He merely understood the implications of this new reality, as quickly as any other owner out there did. Early on, Brad Corbett, owner of the Texas Rangers, and "Cowboy" Gene Autry, the late owner of the Angels, were his main competition.

Number two: George had a tremendous desire to win at all costs. He understood that the Yankees were meant to win. Also, never forget that another Mickey Mantle, there will never be. George knew that he needed Reggie and others combined to put the Yankees "over the top."

George vigorously pursued Reggie. "It was Steinbrenner's sheer relentless persistence," gasped Jackson later. "He hustled me like a broad."

George did his best, and his intentions were often misconstrued. He had certainly made more millionaires than any other baseball owner. Were owners Dan Topping and Del Webb so good to the Yankees?

George's teams always looked good on paper. Some players, however, weren't worth the paper that their contracts were written on.

Pitchers:

Ed Whitson takes the cake. (As opposed to eccentric reliever Sparky Lyle, who literally took the cake and sat on it naked.) Whitson just couldn't pitch with the New York City monkey on his back.

Mike Hampton was certainly in the same class along with Wayne Garland and Denny Neagle.

The one-time Oakland Athletic ace Kenny Holtzman was said to retire "when the ink was still wet." He went 2 – 3 in 1977.

Don Gullett was going to be the next Sandy Koufax. He had a career record of 109 – 50 and was outstanding for the Reds. In 1978, Gullett had a double rotator cuff tear. (His bad luck spiraled downward as he had a heart attack in 1986 and a triple-bypass, at the age of 39, in 1990.)

Doyle Alexander couldn't break a pane of glass with his arm, or more importantly, with his fastball. He was a pathetic 1 – 8 in two years. He went to Toronto and went 17 – 10 on garbage.

Tim Leary was supposed to be a quality starter. He pitched three years and went 9 – 19, (You would need a calculator to figure out how much it cost per loss). He then *improved* to 4 – 10 and later 5 – 6. Moses could have crossed the desert again, waiting for George to get even on him.

Andy "The Real Thing" Messersmith went 0 – 3 in 1978. Jim Kaat, who is a bonafide Hall of Fame candidate and a wonderful announcer today, was on the other side of his excellent career, going 2 – 3 and 0 – 1 for the Yanks. Steve Trout went 0 – 4 with another case of the New York City blues. Eric Plunk was a definite "looks good on paper" type of guy, who also was a big disappointment.

Hideki Irabu hadn't pitched in a year in Japan and was only a .500 pitcher in their "Powder Puff League." In 1998, he did better because of Mel Stottlemyre's keen eye and fine coaching. In 1999, he started slowly, and then Professor Stottlemyre's influence resulted in much better games. Finally, the Yankees dumped off Irabu to the Montreal Expos, at the end of the season and millennium. There was also Jeff Weaver, Carl Pavano, Kei Igawa, Jaret Wright, Rawly Eastwick, Kenny Rogers and Joba Chamberlin. The jury has definitely made their decision on Sonny Gray. He has so much stuff and is so ineffective.

Infielders:

Eric Soderholm was hitting .147, and manager Dick Howser let him hit away instead of bunt in a crucial situation. First baseman Jim Spencer went nuts. Wayne Tolleson "couldn't hit his way out of a paper bag." Bobby Meacham *was* slick at times with the leather but should have added cork to his bat.

Mike Pagliarulo hit a weak .238 in 1986, but that far exceeded ex- slugger John Mayberry's .209 in 1982. Mike Blowers definitely didn't pan out. Dan Pasqua showed a flash and then was a "flash in the pan." Ken Phelps's promise was also very short-lived.

Outfielders:

My favorite candidates were Paul Blair, a one-time excellent Oriole despite just two big postseason hits, and Jimmy "Already Exploded His Cannon in Houston" Wynn. If I recall correctly, Wynn hit a homer in his first Yankee game, and that was his peak in pinstripes. He was a real fine player for Houston, being named the "Toy Cannon." José Altuve is the real "Toy Cannon."

Omar "The Outmaker" Moreno had no punch. Steve Kemp from the Tigers, Dave Collins the ex-Red, and José Cruz bombed as Yankees. Jesse Barfield, the ex-Blue Jays standout, and Danny Tartabull from Kansas City were not much better.

Catchers:

I'm not sure that Rick Cerone and Barry Foote ever looked good on the roster. Cerone was marginal with his defense. Maybe the next Mickey will come along at the same time as the next Thurman Munson. If you're going to dream, why not make it huge?

Designated Hitters:

Jack Clark reminded me of a guess hitter like Joe Adcock. The difference, however, was that Adcock had no enormous contracts and didn't swing from his toes on every pitch. Kevin Maas was another failure as a long-term DH.

Here's hoping that George's sons, Hal and Hank, will confer with real Yankees fans in the future.

THE GREATEST YANKEES

If you're not a real Yankees fan, do not indulge.

So which players, then, do I feel were the most valuable Yankees ever by position? Who were the top assets to their club?

First base:
Lou Gehrig, no disputing this, and Don Mattingly

Second Base:
Joe Gordon, Robinson Cano, Tony Lazzeri, Billy Martin, and Bobby Richardson

Shortstop:
Derek Jeter, no contest, and Phil Rizzuto

Third Base:
Alex Rodriguez. Clete Boyer, and Graig Nettles

Right Field:
Babe Ruth, Roger Maris, Dave Winfield and Hank Bauer

Center Field:
Mickey Mantle and Joe DiMaggio

Left Field:
Charlie Keller and Bob Meusel

Catchers:
Yogi Berra, Bill Dickey, Thurman Munson, Elston Howard, and Jorge Posada

Pitchers:
Whitey Ford, Lefty Grove, Red Ruffing, Allie Reynolds, Andy Pettitte, Vic Raschi, Ron Guidry, Lefty Gomez, Catfish Hunter, and Mel Stottlemyre

Relievers:
Mariano Rivera, and the rest: Goose Gossage, Dave Righetti, Sparky Lyle, and Luis Arroyo

Managers:
Miller Huggins, Joe McCarthy, Casey Stengel, and Joe Torre

Most Valuable Yankee Ranking:
1. Babe Ruth
2. Lou Gehrig
3. Mickey Mantle

4. Joe DiMaggio
5. Yogi Berra
6. Derek Jeter
7. Whitey Ford
8. Mariano Rivera
9. Bill Dickey
10. Roger Maris
11. Thurman Munson
12. Phil Rizzuto
13. Don Mattingly
14. Ron Guidry
15. Andy Pettitte

The "All-Time" Lineup:
1. Derek Jeter
2. Robinson Cano
3. Mickey Mantle
4. Babe Ruth
5. Lou Gehrig
6. Joe DiMaggio
7. Yogi Berra
8. Alex Rodriguez
9. Whitey Ford

DH: Roger Maris   RP: Mariano Rivera

19

THE GREATEST ATHLETE OF THE CENTURY

> *"The perfect baseball player would possess the power of Ruth and Foxx, the speed of Cobb, and the extraordinary fielding abilities of Mays and DiMaggio. The perfect player was Mickey Mantle."*
> – Eddie Lopat, Major League Baseball Manager

Our great nation is once again at peace. Our economy is at an all-time high, allowing baseball to make another comeback, even supporting the ludicrous salaries of today's marketplace. Players are simply commodities. Marketing sports, including baseball, is a new art form, one never that has never been seen to this dimension before.

All the votes are in for the greatest athlete of all time. Lists from ESPN, *Sports Illustrated*, and virtually every other sports publication has placed Muhammad Ali, Michael Jordan, Babe Ruth, Pele, Jim Thorpe, and Jimmy Brown up top. The effort was there. But too often, the creators of these lists focus on creating hype and pleasing advertisers, not defining what it means to be a great athlete.

Are we voting for the person who meant the most to the game as a sports figure? Was this just in the United States or worldwide? Are we talking about true athleticism, or a combination of icon recognition and athleticism? Nobody has ever explained the rules beforehand.

Nor do these polls delve into the real issues of baseball: astronomical salaries, performance-enhancing drugs, and the regulations surrounding the juiced ball, the pitcher's mound, and the designated hitter rule. The choices, too, are often short-sighted.

How could any real baseball fan not include Bill Dickey on their list? And who says that Johnny Bench was better than Yogi Berra was? For those of you who don't have a long perspective on the game, Bill Dickey was even better than Johnny Bench defensively and much more proficient with his bat. Dickey did not have quite the home run power that Bench had but did have power, slugging more than 200 homers in a very expansive Yankee Stadium. He hit against top-notch pitching that delivered a much deader ball compared to those pitched after 1976.

Dickey was a lifetime hitter over 17 seasons of .313! He put the ball in play, striking out nearly 1,000 times less than Bench. Dickey averaged a much higher total of RBIs per at bat than Bench for their entire careers. And you must remember that Dickey hit after the great(s) Lou Gehrig, and Joe DiMaggio, also Charlie Keller, and Tommy "Mr. Dependable" Henrich. How many opportunities were left to drive in runs? Bench hit after all-time hit leader Pete Rose and Hall of Famer Joe Morgan, as a duo got on base more than anyone else in history.

We need to stay educated about our great American pastime. Baseball history should be offered as a college course.

So, who is the "Greatest Athlete"? I believe that the winner should be a multi-talented athlete with a remarkable ability to play many sports. In terms of boxing alone, who says that Ali was better than Rocky Marciano or Joe Louis? Marciano never lost a fight in his career. If you poll the sportswriters, their answer would be Joe Louis. What else could Ali do in terms of athletics?

The Babe was a great athlete. He was a Hall of Fame type pitcher who revolutionized the game. He smashed all records in the dead ball era. He was an excellent marksman, too, and trained for baseball by boxing.

Jim Thorpe was a remarkably talented athlete. He was an outstanding football player, Olympic gold medalist in the pentathlon and decathlon. He was also a world-class high jumper and an average baseball player with a .251 batting average.

Jackie Robinson was also a remarkable athlete. He had a Hall of Fame baseball career against all odds. At UCLA, he displayed exceptional speed as a track man and football player. He was also an excellent tennis player.

My vote, however, goes to Mickey Mantle. He was the most remarkable athlete ever, with a combination of natural ability and discipline on and off the diamond.

In high school, Mantle played basketball and football. As a sophomore, he was spiked in a football game and ended up having osteomyelitis in his left leg. The infection was so bad doctors actually considered amputation. Thank God that antibiotics were discovered that same year in 1935. He came back and played as a senior.

As a halfback in a T-formation and a fullback in a single

wing, he was named to the All-District team, despite having very little experience. In Mickey's words, "I had good hands and could outrun everybody." Once, he tried punting. His first attempt sailed far over the head of the safety, which they were then called. Mickey's high school coach, John Lingo, said that Mickey could have easily received a football scholarship to the college of his choice.

In track, Mickey would have been the equal of Carl Lewis. If Bob Mathias had mentored him, Mickey could have excelled in every event. Mathias stated that "Mickey could have done anything."

And let's not forget that in golf, Mantle had a much longer drive than the great Jack Nicklaus did!

But Mantle's destiny did not lie on the track, the football field, or the golf course. Mickey's father, semi-pro pitcher Elven "Mutt" Mantle, was grooming him for baseball.

Mickey exhibited explosive power and blinding speed; he could put the fear of God into shortstops and second-basemen when breaking up a double play.

According to Casey Stengel, Mickey was the fastest baseball player ever. (He should know – he watched or played alongside so many of them!) Casey told the writers, "There's never been anything like this kid. He has more speed than any slugger and more slug than any speedster – and nobody has ever had more of both of 'em together."

In the outfield, Mickey was mentored by the great "Old Reliable" Tommy Henrich. Tom worked for days with Mickey to teach him how to catch the ball and get rid of it, all in one move. "When Mickey came in," Henrich recalled, "I say, 'You got it down pretty good. I think that's the best throw I ever saw.'"

In his book *Baseball's All Time Dream Team*, John P.

McCarthy rates Mickey better than Ty Cobb for the third starting outfield position of the Dream Outfield Team. After intense statistical scrutiny and introspection, McCarthy cannot find a methodology to convince himself to change this rating. He also lists Mickey as one of the best all-round hitters ever, along with Ruth and Gehrig.

Arguably, hitting a baseball is the most difficult feat in sports, especially under the conditions in which Mickey played. Nobody could hit a ball farther or harder from both sides of the plate. What you may not know is the fact that Mickey's lifetime average right- handed was an astounding .329! That is up there with Williams's lifetime left-handed average and nearly equal to that of the great Joe Jackson, also a lefty. Cobb had the highest average of .366, and he hit left-handed, too. Some argue that hitting right-handed against left- handed pitchers is harder than hitting left-handed against righties.

I have never seen a lefty pitcher who could throw a ball that didn't naturally move. Griffey, Jr., as an outfielder, came close.

Mickey's lifetime right-handed average is not far off from that of great players like Rogers Hornsby at .358. But Hornsby hardly had Mickey's power. Mickey hit more home runs per at bat than Hornsby hit doubles. And Mickey hit more doubles, in fewer at bats, than Hornsby hit homers. Simply put, Mickey was the most proficient right-handed hitter who ever played, and he played in the world's most difficult right-handed hitting park, to boot. His fantastic right-handed average also dispels the ridiculous notion that Yankee Stadium was built for Mickey and enhanced his stats. If it weren't for a crippling right knee during Mickey's last 10 years, his average left- handed would have also been much higher.

New statistics are measured in Sabermetrics. In *The Last*

American Boy, Jane Leavy notes that Mantle finished second behind only Babe Ruth following an analysis of win shares per at bat from sabermetrician Cyril Morong.

Even with bad knees, Mickey had 41 extra-inning home runs, 118 game-winning home runs, and, conservatively speaking, 500 (old) baseballs that traveled more than 420 feet -- including flyouts!

To recap, listed below are just some of Mickey's attributes and accomplishments:

- Exhibited world-class speed with power – a Carl Lewis type
- Was the fastest ever to first base batting left-handed (3.1 seconds official),
- Held the record for all four bases (13 seconds), even though "Cool Papa" Bell allegedly did it in 12 seconds and the "official: record of 13.3 seconds is held by Evar Swanson of the 1931 Reds.
- Broke up a double play like nobody else
- Hit at least one fair ball out of Yankee Stadium and set records in numerous other stadiums, too
- Was a terrific clutch performer, with a record 18 World Series home runs
- Held many other World Series records, such as runs scored, total bases, and RBIs
- Rated number one in the American League under the Total Player Rating (in *Total Baseball*) every year from 1955 to 1962
- Won the Triple Crown and Athlete of the Year and achieved 50 homers in 1956 -- a combination never accomplished by any other player

- Named MVP for three seasons (and could have been for a total of nine, according to Bill James)
- Selected for the hall of Fame in his first year of eligibility, 1974
- Had an exceptional arm, according to experts like Tommy Henrich and Casey Stengel
- Hit more 500- and 600-foot home runs than all other players combined and hit two that could have traveled 700 feet or more
- Hit many 400-yard drives in golf, outdistancing golf greats like Arnold Palmer and Jack Nicklaus
- Was a terrific football player
- Played high school basketball
- Was a good bowler
- Was an excellent hunter and marksman
- Was the second-largest icon in baseball to the Babe

*

Mickey was the consummate perfect 10-tool player. What amazes me is how fast so many fans forget what really great looks like. At least sportswriter and best-selling author Scott Pitoniak can still remember Mickey Mantle's awesome impact on and off the field.

"Mickey was truly one of the greatest stars ever," Pitoniak stated, "possessing six tools (hitting for power, average, tremendous speed, bunting, a fine arm, and outstanding defense)." I would also submit that there was much more: hitting in the clutch, breaking up the double play, being a phenomenal influence on his teammates and leading them to victory in the World Series. He was also a huge ambassador of the game, which actually led the players into free agency as a whole.

1. Hitting for power: Nobody who ever played had more power. His slugging average was surpassed only by Babe Ruth.
2. Average: He had a career batting average just shy of .300 and consistently stayed above that figure for most seasons of his career.
3. Tremendous speed: Nobody was ever faster on the base paths from home to first or around all four bases. He was a great instinctual base runner, like Mays and Aaron. His successful stolen base average was 80 percent.
4. Bunting: Mickey was the best drag bunter in the game and with two strikes also.
5. A fine arm: Mickey had an exceptional arm; very few dared run on him.
6. Outstanding defense: He was a terrific outfielder who could outrun most any flyball and had great instincts.
7. Hitting in the clutch: Mickey was the ultimate clutch hitter. He hit homers off outstanding pitchers, such as Warren Spahn, Billy Loes, Joe Black, Preacher Roe, Johnny Padres, Sal Maglie, Bob Buhl, Sandy Koufax, Bob Gibson and many others.
8. Breaking up the double play: He was the best at breaking up a double play based on his speed of getting to second and the intense power packed in his slide.
9. Being a phenomenal influence on his teammates: Mickey was truly inspirational. According to former teammates Bobby Richardson, Tony Kubek, Clete Boyer, and Bobby Murcer, everyone would be inspired

to "play up" just from seeing Mickey in the clubhouse. No doubt, this strategy helped lead the team to seven World Series victories.

10. Serving as an ambassador for the game: Mickey's influence helped overturn the reserve clause, which made everyone who followed filthy rich based on their skill level I defy anyone to name a more talented athlete in the last 100 years than the incomparable legend Mickey Mantle. If you have a different opinion after reading all 2,401 box scores and countless more articles, I would enjoy your perspective.

Mickey was simply the best at every element of the game, and the pros knew it, too. Once, a youngster stopped the great Al Kaline after the game and said, "Mr. Kaline, you're not one-half as good as Mickey Mantle."

Kaline turned to the kid and said, "Son, *nobody* is one-half as good as Mickey Mantle."

20

THE NEXT MURDERERS' ROW & THE FUTURE OF BASEBALL

"A team is where a boy can prove his courage on his own. A gang is where a coward goes to hide."
– Mickey Mantle

Baseball talks are a blast because people come charging at you with their opinion. "I hated Mantle; Mays was so much better." Everyone has the right to their own opinion and criteria, even if their knowledge base is shallow.

I fell in love with baseball when I was five years old and saw Willie Mays make his remarkable catch is the 1954 World Series. Vic Wertz was the batter. The Yankees captivated me because the Game of the Week on national TV was nearly always the Yankees. How could you not fall in love with Mickey, Whitey, and Yogi, unless you wanted to lose?

The year 1961 was a magical one in the baseball world. "The Chase" was so exciting. Mickey, the fan favorite, and Roger Maris chased Babe Ruth's record of 60 home runs in a single season. There was limited access to coverage before ESPN and computers.

The newspapers where the primary source of information. Most games where not on TV. Transistor radios carried some of the games, but often the transmission was not consistently audible. It was a great time for avid baseball fans to use their vivid imaginations based on radio announcers' descriptions of play.

What a great line-up: Bobby, Tony, Roger, Mickey, Yogi, Elston, Moose, Clete, and Whitey! The catching rotation of Yogi, Elston Howard, and Johnny Blanchard produced 63 homers! They won 109 games and won the World Series in five games, even with Mickey's limited presence because of a nasty bleeding abscess on his hip. This team is often mentioned as a candidate for the greatest team in baseball history. That, in my opinion, was the second iteration of Murderers' Row. The term "Murderers' Row" describes the baseball teams of the New York Yankees in the late 1920s, widely considered among the best lineups in the team's history. Most commonly, this moniker applies to the first six hitters in the 1927 team lineup: Earle Combs, Mark Koenig, Babe Ruth, Lou Gehrig, Bob Meusel, and Tony Lazzeri. The 1927 Yankees were one of the best teams ever, dominating their opponents and winning 110 of 152 games.

The 1920s were a different era of baseball. The balls, the fences, and the bats were very different. However, eras cannot be compared, only enjoyed.

The closest we've come to Murderers' Row since the 1960s was the 1998 New York Yankees team. In 1998, the Yankees won a record 114 regular season games and the World Series. Star player Derek Jeter had over 200 hits and a batting average of .324. Other standout players included Bernie Williams, Tino Martinez, Paul O'Neill, Jorge Posada, Scott Brosius, Chad Curtiss, Darryl Strawberry, Chuck Knoblauch, and Joe Girardi.

Undoubtedly, some will argue that this was the best team in history, albeit not a homer-leading club with a big horse in the race. Their rotation was a "thing of beauty." Led by David Cone's 20 wins and then David Wells, Andy Pettitte, Orlando "El Duque" Hernández, and Hideki Irabu. The Bullpen was fabulous: Mariano "Mo" Rivera, Ramiro Mendoza, Mike Stanton, Jeff Nelson, and Graeme Lloyd. However, they were no Murderers' Row. They were the "Pinstripe Machine."

Do you think that there will ever be another Ruth/Gehrig, or for that matter Mantle/Maris, combination again? If you say yes, it will be a creation of free agency, not one of homegrown origins. You can trade statistics, but the culture and mystique of the Yankees goes far beyond money. Some acquisitions do emulate Yankee pride by virtue of their personalities and are a perfect fit. Catfish pitching to a home-grown Thurman Munson was perfect, O'Neill's intensity and all-out hustle emulates Hank Bauer in right, and David Cone always looked like a Yankee in the fashion of Whitey Ford.

That's not to say, however, that it couldn't happen again. The 2018 Yankees could be contenders for the next Murderers' Row if they stay healthy. Players to watch: Giancarlo Stanton, with 59 home runs; Aaron Judge, with 52; Gary Sanchez, who hit 33 homers after missing two months of play; and Greg Bird, a true slugger.

But any Yankee historian would be remiss if they did not highlight the Yankees of the late 1930s. What a fantastic line-up: Crosetti, Rolfe, Henrich, DiMaggio, Gehrig, Dickey, Selkirk and Joe Gordon. Young Joe DiMaggio drove in over 500 runs in his first four years!

The Yankee team today maybe a team of destiny, not dynasty. If you don't believe me, you can look it up.

EPILOGUE

Mickey Mantle: An Appreciation by Scott Pitoniak
Best-selling author and nationally honored journalist

During the endless summers of our youth, we would slide our baseball gloves onto the handlebars of our bikes and head to the neighborhood park where we played ball from sunrise to sunset.

We would arrange our bikes in the outfield to conform to the strange configuration of Yankee Stadium. We would make it ridiculously short in right, impossibly deep in center. And then we would draw straws to see who would get to be Mickey Mantle that day.

It was the early 1960s, a time when the Beatles invaded our shores and record stores for the first time, JFK inspired a nation to explore a New Frontier, and baseball served as our national pastime instead our national pass-time.

In those days, millions of us Baby Boomers wanted to be just like the Mick. He gripped our souls the way his powerful hands once gripped a Louisville Slugger.

We wanted to wear the regal New York Yankee pinstripes with the No. 7 on the broad back and roam the expansive, lush green outfield of the world's most famous ballpark. In our sandlot games, we would swing so hard from both sides of the plate in hope of making baseballs get small in a hurry, just like the Mick. Some of us were so into Mantle we even imitated his gimpy-kneed home run trot. Head down. Arms up.

One of the highlights of our youthful springs was ripping open a pack of baseball cards and finding a Mantle nestled between a Bill Tuttle and a "Daddy Wags" Wagner. We didn't need a price guide to tell us his card was valuable. Our hearts told us so.

We kept scrapbooks of his heroics, pored over box scores in search of his name in the morning paper, and sneaked transistor radios into classrooms to listen to the World Series exploits of the original Mr. October.

These eyes have had the privilege of seeing many sports icons perform up-close and personal. We have watched Michael Jordan defy the laws of gravity, Joe Montana and Tom Brady turn a pressure- packed Super Bowl into a leisurely backyard game of pitch and catch, and the Golden Bear drain a 60-foot birdie putt during a U.S. Open.

But none of these athletes, none of these moments, ever thrilled us the way Mickey taking batting practice did during the summer of '66. We were only 11 at the time, but impression is indelible. It was our first trip to the House that Ruth Built and Mantle Renovated. As we watched in awed amazement while the blonde-haired, biceps- bulging Mantle muscled batting practice offerings into the clouds, we couldn't help but notice a different sound to the balls he hit. It was an explosion rather that a *crack* of the bat. White ash against horsehide never sounded so good.

All these memories came rushing back when the idol of our youth fought a courageous but losing battle against liver cancer. Mantle's life, by his own admission, was flawed. He had endured tragedy -- some of it beyond his control, some of it self-induced. But he never sought pity, and he never blamed anyone but himself. And those who worshipped him unconditionally in our youth came to admire him even more during the final 18 months of his life.

As the most gifted natural athlete to ever play the game, Mantle had often saved his best for the late innings. And so, it was with his life.

He talked with amazing candor and poignancy about his 42-year struggle with alcoholism in hopes that others wouldn't follow the same path. He attempted to reconcile differences with his family, to be a father he rarely was when his boys were young.

And in a gesture more powerful than any of the 536 home runs he had blasted during his 18-year Hall of Fame career, he threw his name and energies behind a national organ and tissue donor campaign. The liver transplant that prolonged his life so moved Mantle that he insisted on doing all that he could to raise public awareness about the importance of organ and tissue donations.

Hemingway described courage as "grace under pressure," and in the final weeks of Mantle's life, he embodied that definition. His doctors said he was, in many ways, the most remarkable patient they had ever seen. His bravery was so stark and real that even those used to see people in dire circumstances were touched by his example. Organ donations rose dramatically all across America. Mick had homered again.

In an eloquent, passionate eulogy at Mantle's funeral, NBC broadcaster Bob Costas talked of the ballplayer's greatness and vulnerability from the pulpit of a suburban Dallas church:

> "He had those dual qualities so seldom seen, exuding dynamism and excitement but at

the same time touching your heart -- flawed, wounded. We know there was something poignant about Mickey Mantle before we knew what 'poignant' meant. We just didn't root for him, we felt for him.

"Long before any of us cracked a serious book, we knew something about mythology as we watched Mickey Mantle run out a home run through the lengthening shadows of a late Sunday afternoon at Yankee Stadium....

"I just hope God has a place for him where he can run again. Where he can play practical jokes on his teammates and smile that boyish smile 'cause God knows, no one is perfect. And God knows there's something special about heroes."

It's been nearly more than six decades since Mick came to Rochester, New York, to receive the Hickok Belt, the Academy Awards of sports. The endless summer of our youth may have ended, but the special memories of a childhood hero endure.

APPENDIX

Mickey's Phenomenal Career

"If you don't believe me, you can look it up!"

All data and quotes are from the Rochester Democrat and Chronicle. The articles researched span from April 1, 1951, to March 1, 1968. These are the actual dates of the games. The article excerpts appeared the next morning.

The Democrat and Chronicle has a special place in my heart. I learned how to read the box scores in this newspaper when I was about six years old. At age seven, I was watching Mickey's progress on his Triple Crown, towards the end of the year. In 1961, when I was 12, I would rip open the sports section to "watch" Mickey and Roger's chase of Babe Ruth's home run record. To this day, I read the sports section first.

1951

April 1: Spring training. Mickey is called a "Sensational Rookie." He has three hits against Pittsburgh in Phoenix.

April 8: In Houston, "belted" a three-run homer "out of the park."

April 9: "The Rookie hits like DiMaggio and runs like the speed of light. No rookie since Musial (1941) was this impressive."

April 10: Faces the home Draft Board.

April 12: According to reports, "Would go into the Army and serve, if drafted."

April 13: Rejected by the Army based on osteomyelitis from a high school football injury.

April 15: Called a "once-in-a-lifetime rookie" by the Associated Press. April 15: In New York, four hits in an exhibition game vs. the Dodgers, including a home run.

April 16: Called "a Rookie Phenom"

April 17: Opening Day in New York. Mickey plays in his first Major League game, a single, against the Red Sox.

April 18: In New York, hits a two-run single

April 20: In Washington, D.C., plays a double-header in front of President Truman

April 21: In D.C., drives in the winning run.

April 23: In New York, "Mickey led team" along with DiMaggio; each goes three for five.

May 1: In Chicago, Mickey hits his first home run, a "440-foot shot," off Randy Gumpert of the Chicago White Sox.

May 2: Sprained his left hand.

May 4: In St. Louis at Sportsman Park, "Mantle boomed his second HR, zoomed over the right field pavilion on Grand Avenue."

May 6: In Detroit, collects three hits.

May 10: Reported to be among the league RBI leaders. May 12: In Philadelphia, collects three hits.

May 13: In Philadelphia, hit his third homer.

May 16: Among the RBI leaders, hits his fourth home run. May 18: In New York, collects three hits, including a triple. May 20: Becomes the American League RBI leader.

June 1: Casey reported that he sprained his left hand and may get benched; still the AL RBI leader.

June 3: Plays a doubleheader in Cleveland with 75,163 in attendance. June 19: In New York, hit a three-run homer.

June 20: In New York, the Yankees win 2 – 1. "Mickey pegs out a runner at third base, by a mile," from right field.

July 5: "Mickey has a 'rifle arm' and fields with the sureness of Tris Speaker."

July 15: "Casey sends Mickey down to Kansas City for more seasoning. Orders the manager to play him exclusively in center field."

August 2: Receives second Draft Board notice.

August 20: Recalled to the Yankees. In 40 games in the minors, Mickey hit .364, 11 HR, and 50 RBIs.

August 24: Turned down by the Army for the third time.

August 25: In Cleveland, hits a "tremendous 2-run homer."

September 8: In New York, hits his 10th home run: "a 450-foot homer into the right field stands to break up the game."

September 13: In New York, "slams the first pitch of the game for a home run off Virgil Trucks."

September 19: In New York, "Mickey has one of only two Yankee hits to win and keep a three-percentage point lead in the pennant race."

October 5: At Yankee Stadium, Game Two of the World Series. Mickey sustains a serious right knee injury on a ball hit by Willie Mays.

1952

March 19: Hit home runs in Clearwater. April 4: In Atlanta, "blasts a homer."

April 8: "Seen as DiMaggio's replacement."

April 16: Opening Day in Philadelphia "booms three hits and plays right field."

April 21: In New York, hits his first homer of the year. May 6: Mickey's father passes away at 40 years old.

May 13: In Cleveland, plays third base.

May 18: In St. Louis, is back in center field.

May 20: In Chicago, has a four-hit game.

June 17: In Detroit, hits a home run into the upper left-center bleachers.

July 1: Named to his first All-Star team.

July 13: In New York, hits a homer in both ends of a doubleheader.

July 15: In New York, "wallops" a home run.

July 17: "Slams a tremendous blast into the upper right field deck at Yankee Stadium."

July 26: In Detroit, hits his first grand slam.

July 29: In Chicago, hits another grand slam.

August 9: In New York, makes "a great throw to the plate from center field [and] nails the runner."

August 11: In New York, hits two homers in a game.

September 21: Receives his third Army physical.

October 2: World Series Game Two; hits a "tremendous blast" off the scoreboard at Ebbets Field for a double.

October 6: At Ebbets Field, "hits a tremendous ball" into the center-field stands.

October 7: At Ebbets Field, hits home run to win the World Series. Jackie Robinson said, "They didn't miss DiMaggio, Mantle killed us."

October 28: Receives decision on the draft and is turned down once more for the Army.

1953

March 9: Hits a 425-foot home run at spring training in Sarasota. March 11: In Orlando, hits a homer.

March 12: Reaches .444 average. March 14: Hits a home run in Miami.

April 9: Drives the ball out of Forbes Field in Pittsburgh, becoming the third player ever to accomplish this feat after Ted Beard and Babe Ruth (714th home run).

April 17: Hits an "astounding" 562- to 565-foot homer off Chuck Stobbs in Washington.

April 21: In New York, "a perfect peg to third base erases runner."

April 22: In New York, "a blast off Ellis Kinder travels 420 feet into the right field bleachers."

April 29: "Blasts a home run shot in Chicago, which goes into the bleachers and rebounded back into the field."

May 8: "Blasts one off the Fenway light tower in left field."

June 10: Hits in 16 straight games and "slams a ball off the roof at Briggs Stadium, Detroit," off Art Houtteman.

June 14: Hit streak reaches 20.

July 6: "Hits a tremendous grand slam" in Philadelphia.

September 12: Hits his third 500-foot home run of the season, vs. Detroit at Yankee Stadium, the third ever hit into the third left-field deck in nine years.

October 1: In New York, "belts" a World Series home run.

October 4: With the World Series tied at two games each, hits a "spectacular" grand slam at Ebbets Field. One reporter said that there was "never a prettier sight" of a ball in flight.

October: Named to the AL MVP Team.

1954

April 10: Plays his first spring training game after rehabbing his right knee, which was operated on again.

April 18: In New York, hits a 470-foot triple.

July 2: Ranks first in home runs, third in RBIs, and sixth in BA in the American League.

July 3: Named the starting center fielder in the All-Star game.

July 28: Game-winning home run into the center-field stands in Chicago in the ninth inning.

August 5: Hits two home runs in Cleveland; the second travels into the upper right-field seats, a rare feat.

August 9: At Doubleday Field, Cooperstown, "Mickey hit a homer off the roof of a house behind the left field fence" against Cincinnati. September 2: In New York, hits a tremendous 450-foot drive for a home run.

September 26: In New York, Mickey plays shortstop in the Yankees' final game.

1955

March 14: In Bradenton, Mickey hits a grand slam and drives in six off the Braves.

March 29: In Lakeland, scores a home run against the Tigers. April 4: Hitting a .346 BA.

April 5: Hits the game-winning home run in Knoxville, Tennessee.

April 6: In Lynchburg, Virginia, hits a home run.

April 7: Red Smith said, "Even money that Willie Mays doesn't beat Mickey Mantle in two of these three departments: total hits, run-batted-in, batting average."

April 8: In Wilmington, Delaware, Mickey hits an inside-the-park homer against the Phillies.

April 13: In New York, Mickey hits a homer on Opening Day. The Yankees romp 19 – 1 over Washington.

May 13: In New York, blasts 3 homers in a game, both sides.

May 22: In New York, reaches base 15 consecutive times.

May 27: In Baltimore, "rips a 400-foot double and 400-foot triple."

May 28: In Baltimore, ball flies out to Diering 440 feet away.

June 3: In Chicago, "smashes a prodigious wallop into left center for a homer."

June 5: In Chicago, hits a home run off of Billy Pierce: "a tremendous blast which hit the base of the light tower on the upper deck roof in left field."

June 6: "Clouts another tape-measure blast in Detroit, over the screen in dead center just right of the 440 sign. The veteran press box couldn't remember anyone that had cleared the 12-foot screen."

June 17: "Lofts a tremendous shot off Donovan" in New York.

June 21: In Yankee Stadium, "blasts one of the longest homers ever. The ball hit off Kellner of Kansas City, left the yard at the 461-foot sign and cleared the 30-foot barrier in deep center field." The press calls it a 461- foot homer!

July 3: Mickey is named to the All-Star team as the starting center fielder.

July 9: Goes five-for-five against Washington.

July 10: In Washington, hits three home runs into the distant bleachers in a doubleheader.

July 12: In the All-Star game in Milwaukee, hits a 425-foot homer at the base of the wall. The "screaming" hit cleared a double fence and rolled towards a cluster of trees.

Leo Durocher said that the wind was blowing in and just shook his head.

August 4: "Smashes a homer into the upper deck in right field" in Yankee Stadium.

August 7: "Hits one into the upper stands in right field" in Yankee Stadium to win the game.

August 15: In Baltimore, "blasts two circuit clouts." Goes 5-8 in a DH, drives in 5.

August 16: Hits a "jarring blow" at Fenway Park.

August 19: "Smashed his 31st homer off the third deck" at Yankee Stadium vs. Baltimore.

August 24: Hits the upper right-field deck at Briggs Stadium, going back to back with Yogi's like shot in the ninth inning, to secure a 3 – 2 win in a critical pennant chase game.

December: Wins the official HR and Slugging titles of the American League.

1956: The Triple Crown Year

March 17: At spring training in St. Petersburg, Florida, hits a homer that leaves the yard at 420 feet.

March 20: In St. Petersburg, a homer leaves the yard at 450 feet.

March 21: In St. Petersburg, "wallops" a 475-foot homer and a 450-foot triple.

March 24: In Miami, hits "a tremendous line-drive home run which cleared the center field wall at 400 feet and 30 feet high by several feet."

April 12: In Cincinnati, "a towering drive sailed high over the right- centerfield wall beyond the 390-foot sign"; also hit a "towering 380-foot shot" and a total of six in the Grapefruit League.

April 17: Opening Day in Washington with President Eisenhower watching. "Mickey Mantle today became the first man in baseball history to blast two home runs in a single game over the far away center-field fence in Griffith Stadium (off Camilo Pascual, a right-hander). Mickey drove pitches high over the 30-foot wall. The first homer bounced off a roof across the street. The second soared over the 438 mark and carried into a tree."

April 21: At Yankee Stadium, hits his fourth home run of the year, "which sailed about 100 feet in the air over the 415-foot marker."

May 5: "Clouts two homers at Yankee Stadium" and leads the league in HRs (9), RBIs (23) and BA (.433).

May 18: In New York, hits both right-handed and left-handed home runs.

May 21: In Kansas City, hits a home run over two fences, up a 40-foot embankment, and out of the park.

May 24: Goes five-for-five against Detroit, including his 17th home run in New York.

May 30: In New York, "raps a pair of homers in a doubleheader against Washington. Batting lefty against Pedro Ramos, the mammoth drive lacked only 8 inches of finding a clear path out of Yankee Stadium. The ball was hit 117 feet high at the 370-foot mark. Frank Crosetti and Bill Dickey both played with Ruth and Gehrig and saw Foxx, Greenberg, Williams, and all others play agreed that they never saw a ball travel farther. The second homer cracked the bleacher seats in right-center."

June 14: In New York, "The blast left the park at the 420 mark in right- center."

June 18: In Detroit, "Another tape-measure home run off Paul Foytack. Hitting left-handed, the blast, which was hit against the wind, sailed onto the roof at Briggs Stadium and took a bounce onto Trumbull Avenue. The ball traveled well over the 370-foot mark and 110 feet high. Mickey was only the second man ever to leave the stadium that opened in 1937. Ted Williams did it as a rookie on May 4, 1939."

June 20: In Detroit, off Billy Hoeft, Mickey hits two "tremendous homers."

July 1: In New York against Washington, hits a pair in a doubleheader. Home run number 28 travels into the third deck in left field; number 29 "soars into the right field bullpen."

July 7: "Announces that he will probably sit out of the All-Star game due to a torn ligament in his right knee."

July 10: Plays all nine innings of the All-Star game and hits a homer off Warren Spahn.

July 14: In New York, home run number 30 "leaves the yard at 440 feet into the left field stands" against Cleveland.

July 30: Smashes two homers in Cleveland; number 33 is a Grand Slam. This is the sixth time this year that Mickey hit two homers in one game.

August 4: In Detroit, "raps out two more homers in one game again."

August 5: Hits home run number 37 in Detroit off Bunning, "a towering drive which slams off the facade of the upper right-field deck."

August 8: "Slams" number 38 in Washington.

August 9: "Belts" number 39 in New York "into the left-field bleachers."

August 15: "Clouts" number 42 "deep into the left-field seats."

August 24: "Hits a 457-foot triple, a bunt and a shot into the upper left-field seats."

August 28: In New York, "wallops number 45 into the bullpen in right-center."

August 31: In Washington, "a clout far over the right-field fence," with President Eisenhower there again.

September 17: Ted Williams surpasses Mickey in batting average.

September 18: In Chicago off lefty Billy Pierce, blasts home run number 50 off the upper deck in deep left field. Mickey's homer clinches the pennant."

September 21: Hits home number 51 against Boston at Fenway; the ball travels "at least 480 feet."

September 23: "Inches past Ted Williams in batting average." September 30: Wins the Triple Crown: 52 HR, 130 RBI, .353 BA.

October 3: Hits a World Series homer in Ebbets Field.

October 8: Don Larsen pitches a perfect World Series game. Mickey homers for one of the two Yankee runs. Mickey makes a splendid running catch in deep left-center to save the perfect game. The Yankees go up 3 – 2 in games. The Yankees win in seven games.

October 14: Named to the Sporting News All-Star team.

October 20: Wins the official Slugging Award again, .705.

October 24: Named the United Press All-Star -- a unanimous top choice gathering all 58 votes. Yogi earns 57 votes.

October 30: Wins the Baseball Writer's AP Press All-Star vote.

November 14: Named the MVP of the American League (officially).

December 22: Named the AP Athlete of the Year.

1957

January 21: Wins the prestigious Hickok Belt Award over all other professional athletes.

March 15: During spring training in St. Petersburg, "unloads a 425-foot homer batting lefty."

March 17: In St. Petersburg, "clouts a 420-foot homer."

March 19: "Belts one off Spahn" in Bradenton, Florida.

April 7: "Hits a long triple after missing a week with a bad foot."

April 9: In Jacksonville, hits home run number five for the season. April 10: In Savannah, hits home run number six.

April 11: In Richmond, ends spring training with seven HRs.

April 24: In New York, "smashes" a home run in the eighth inning against the Orioles; Yankees win 3 – 2.

May 20: In Ebbets Field for the Annual Mayor's Trophy Game, "blasts a two-run homer in the 11th inning which holds up." Mickey is hitting .356 with 7 HRs.

May 28: Goes four-for-six and raises his average to .371.

June 11: In Chicago, "smashes" number 15, an upper-deck shot.

June 12: Has hit seven home runs in eight games; "clouts a pair of homers in Chicago, of which one flew over the 425-feet sign, into the bullpen."

June 22: In New York, hits number 20.

June 23: In New York, is now batting .392.

July 1: Hits home run in the 10th inning to beat Baltimore; makes the All- Star Team, starting in center field.

July 4: In New York, "makes a spectacular catch" of a long drive from Dick Gernert of the Red Sox.

July 5: Collects his $1,000^{th}$ hit.

July 8: At Busch Stadium, Mickey bats fourth in front of Ted Williams and plays center field. The starting pitcher is Jim Bunning, the best in the AL.

July 11: In Kansas City, "hits the winning homer off Tom Morgan in the 11th inning."

July 23: In New York, "Mickey hits for the cycle. The walloped tape- measured homer goes at least 465 feet into the right-center bullpen."

July 26: Hits career home run number 200.

July 29: Draws an intentional walk, number 18, which breaks the AL mark; Mickey finishes with number 23 and Ted Williams finishes with 33.

August 3: Hits home run number 38.

August 10: Goes four-for-five and hits and his 31st and longest home run ever in Baltimore's Memorial Stadium, over the 450-foot mark over a hedge in center field and another 25 feet over a wire fence. "Mickey puts on a display of speed and power. He also had a drag bunt and his 15th steal."

August 13: In Boston, "boomed his 32nd HR, a towering line-drive over 400 feet into the right field pavilion. 35,647 fans, the largest crowd of the year sat in awe!"

August 14: In Boston, "belts" home run number 33.

September 9: Has bad shin splints and stays in the hospital for four days. This will plague him through the World Series.

November 6: Named the AP All-Star team center fielder

November 22: Beats out Ted Williams for the title of AL MVP.

1958

March 20: During spring training in St. Petersburg, hits a "pair of tape- measured home runs" and is batting .344.

April 1: In Tampa, hits his fifth home run.

April 12: In New York, "crashes" two home runs against Philadelphia.

May 17: In D.C., "makes a spectacular running stab of Julio Becquer's liner in the ninth inning to save the game 6 – 5. Two runners were on base."

June 6: In New York, "blasts" two home runs.

June 28: Named to the All-Star team.

July 1: In Baltimore, "hits a game-winning blast in the eighth inning."

July 3: "Raps a pair of homers" (numbers 17 and 18) in Washington. The first cleared the 31-foot high barrier in right field by 25 feet; the second landed 20 rows up in the left-centerfield bleachers.

July 5: In New York against Boston, sends the game into extra innings with a ninth inning homer

July 11: In New York vs. Cleveland, Mantle's "towering solo shot" into the upper right-field stands helped win the game.

July 14: In New York vs. Chicago, "wallops his 23rd" into the left-field bleachers batting left-handed.

July 24: In New York, "hits a tremendous wallop off Bunning into the upper right centerfield bleachers over the 415 sign" for homer number 26.

August 12: In New York vs. Baltimore, "blasts" number 33 to take over the HR lead, raising his average to .308.

August 16: In Boston, "smashes" 34th home run into the right-field seats.

August 17: In Boston, "blasts a three-run homer," number 35.

August 22: Hits 36th home run in New York.

September 17: Hits his 41st home run off Jim Bunning who brushed him back, which flies out of Briggs Stadium and across Trumbull Avenue, hitting about 30 feet high on a building across the street – despite a "pretty stiff wind blowing in," according to the AP wire.

September 24: In Boston, hits homer number 42.

September 27: Regains the Home Run Title 42 – 41 against Rocky Colavito, hits .314, and drives in 97.

October 2: In Milwaukee, World Series Game 2, hits two homers.

October 12: Named to the AL All-Star team.

October 30: Named to the AP All-Star team.

1959

March 13: In Lakeland for spring training, hits a home run.

March 26: In St. Petersburg, hits a home run.

April 4: In St. Petersburg, Mickey homers.

April 12: In New York, "blasts a home run into the bullpen."

April 23: In Washington, hits home run number two, which "clears the right-field wall."

May 30: In Washington, goes 5 – 8 in a doubleheader, raising his average to .331.

June 3: In Detroit, "hits a towering game-winning home run in the ninth," his 10th of the season.

June 17: In New York vs. Chicago, "hits a tremendous fly", which lands about nine rows deep in the upper right-field deck -- number 14.

June 18: In New York, hits his 15th home run in the 10th inning to win the game.

June 22: In Kansas City, drives in six with two homers and a triple.

June 23: In Kansas City, hits home run number 18 and has 46 RBIs.

July 3: Named to the AL All-Star team.

July 19: In New York, "hits a 457-foot ground rule double."

September 10: In New York, collects five hits, including number 28.

September 10: In New York, Mickey goes five-for-six against A's.

December 11: Roger Maris gets traded to the Yankees.

December 23: Has the best fielding average, .995, and misses only two of 375 chances.

1960

March: Mickey holds out from spring training for two weeks.

April 10: In Sarasota, hits a 430-foot triple.

April 14: In Richmond, hits his third homer -- the first time Roger and Mickey hit one in the same game.

May 13: In Washington, hits a mighty homer off Jim Kaat high over the right-field 31-foot barrier. Only three others had ever done this.

June 8: Hits two home runs in New York.

June 18: In Chicago, "mammoth" eighth homers by Mickey and Roger. Mickey's 14th sails into the center-field bullpen. Roger's travels into the right-field upper deck

June 21: In Detroit, Mickey hits two homers off the Yankees' nemesis Frank Larry.

July 4: In Washington, hits his 20th home run for the season and 300th of his career. Roger has 25 home runs.

July 5: "Pedro Ramos intentionally hits Mickey with a pitch and gets fined by the league."

July 6: In Baltimore, Mickey "hits a booming triple"; Roger hits number 27.

July 11: Plays in the All-Star game.

July 15: In Detroit, "hits a towering drive for a three-run homer."

July 18: In New York, "hits a shot deep over the left field fence" for home run number 22; Roger hits his 29th.

July 20: In New York, Mickey and Roger "go deep," hitting their 23rd and 31st home runs, respectively.

July 24: In Chicago, Mickey "hammered his 24th into the upper deck in right field."

July 26: In New York, hits his 25th home run of the season.
July 28: In New York, bats sixth and his number 26.

August 6: In Kansas City, Mickey goes four-for-five; Roger hits numbers 34 and 35.

August 13: Mickey "drives a long sacrifice fly to score Roger"; the Yankees win 1 – 0.

August 15: In New York, Mickey "blasts a pair of two-run homers against Baltimore. The Yankees win 4 – 3, regaining first place. Mickey's performance is called a magnificent show."

August 31: In New York, "hits a tremendous triple."

September 6: In New York, "wallops a home run deep into the center field bleachers" for home run number 32.

September 10: In Detroit, hits home run number 33: "Mickey clears the top of the right field stands of Foytack. This is only the third time it was ever accomplished."

September 11: In Cleveland, breaks a tie with homer number 34 in the 11th inning. Roger hits number 38.

September 17: In New York, hits number 37 off Ramos.

September 24: In Boston, hits number 38 in the 10th inning, the game- winning hit.

September 28: In D.C., "Slams two home runs into distant left field seats."

October 2: Wins the HR crown 40 – 39 over Roger.

October 6: In Game 2 of the World Series in Pittsburgh, hits two homers, one of which travels over the 460-foot part of the center-field wall. Mickey has 13 career World Series homers, just two behind Babe Ruth.

October 8: Game 3 in New York, "hits another tape-measured homer."

October: Yankees fire Casey Stengel after Series loss and hire Ralph Houk.

November 9: Roger Maris wins the MVP Award over Mickey by three votes. (Mickey actually received two more first place votes than Roger.) Roger had .283 BA, .581 slugs, 39 HRs, 112 RBIs and led the league in slugs and RBIs. Mickey had .276 BA, .558 slugs, 40 HRs, and 94 RBIs. He led the league in runs (119), home runs, OB percentage, and total bases and was second in walks with 14 steals.

1961

February 26: Houk designates Mickey the leader of the Yankees.

March 15: During spring training in Bradenton, "whacks two homers and 6 RBIs" for four HRs to date.

March 24: Is hitting .526, with 5 HRs and a hitting streak of 13-for-17.

April 8: In St. Louis, hits number seven.

April 20: In New York, hits a pair of homers in a doubleheader.

April 21: In Baltimore, hits the ball over the 380-foot sign.

April 26: In Detroit, "Mickey hits one right and one lefty, the second one a two-run shot in the 10th inning for a game winner." Roger hits a homer.

April 27: In New York, "Mickey hits a 407-foot triple to win the game. This is the fifth game of the year that he won with a long hit."

May 2: In Minnesota, Mickey hits a grand slam in the 10th inning, the game winning hit. "The ball travels over the 430-foot mark in center field."

May 3: In Minnesota, the Yankees bomb Ramos. Mickey has eight homers and a 15-game hitting streak. Roger hits his second home run for the season.

May 4: In Minnesota, Mickey hits number nine and stretches his streak to 16.

May 19: Roger hits homer number five in Cleveland.

May 20: Roger hits homer number six in Cleveland.

May 21: In New York, Roger hits homer number seven.

May 24: In New York, Roger hits homer number eight.

May 30: In Boston, Mickey and Roger both hit two homers; Mickey drives in four runs.

May 31: Mickey and Roger both score home runs in Boston. June 2: In Chicago, Roger hits a homer.

June 3: In Chicago, Roger hits another homer. June 4: In Chicago, Roger hits number 15.

June 5: In New York, Mickey hits number 15.

June 7: In New York, Roger "blasts" number 17.

June 9: In New York, the "M&M Boys' bats boom"; Roger hits number 18 and Mickey hits a homer with four RBIs.

June 10: In New York, Mickey hits a homer and a triple.

June 11: Two games in New York; the first, Roger makes two spectacular catches, Mickey blasts a homer, and in the second Roger hits his 19th and 20th home runs.

June 13: In Cleveland, Roger hits number 21.

June 14: In Cleveland, Roger hits number 22.

June 15: In Cleveland, Mickey hits a home run.

June 17: In Detroit, Mickey and Roger both hit home runs.

June 18: In Detroit, Roger hits number 24.

June 19: In Kansas City, Roger hits number 25.

June 20: In Kansas City, Roger hits number 26.

June 21: In Kansas City, Mickey "skyrockets" two home runs.

June 22: In Kansas City, Roger hits number 27 and two doubles. June 26: In Los Angeles, Mickey hits a homer.

June 28: In Los Angeles, Mickey hits number 24 over the left center-field wall.

June 30: In New York, Mickey hits home run number 25, a tie-breaking 440-foot shot off the center-field wall. Roger hits a double and 3 RBIs.

July 1: In D.C., Roger hits number 28. Mickey hits his 1,000th RBI and two home runs. The first travels over the left-field bleachers and the 457-foot sign – the 12th time in history the ball hit that area. The second is a 450- foot home run.

July 2: In New York, Roger hits numbers 29 and 30 against Washington. Mickey hits number 28.

July 4: In New York, Roger hits number 31 in 77 games.

July 5: In New York vs. Cleveland, Roger hits number 32.

July 8: In New York, Mickey hits number 29.

July 9: In New York, Roger hits number 33.

July 13: In Chicago, Mickey hits number 30, "a shot that traveled some 475 feet and landed in the upper deck in right-center field." Mickey has 350 career home runs. Roger hits a home run off the second deck railing.

July 14: In Chicago, Mickey "lines his 31st into the left-field stands."

July 15: In Chicago, Roger hits number 35 and a triple.

July 16: In Baltimore, Mickey hits number 32 and doubles in a run. The Yankees win 2 – 1.

July 17: In Baltimore, a doubleheader, Mickey hits number 33. The second game M&M both hit one, but the game gets rained out in the top of the fifth inning. Mickey and Roger lose these second-game homers.

July 18: In D.C., Mickey hits two homers to tie Roger at 35.

July 19: In D.C., Mickey hits number 36.

July 21: In Boston, M&M both hit one each: Mickey's 37th, Roger's 36th.

July 25: In Chicago, in a doubleheader, Roger hits four homers to total 40. Mickey hits number 38.

July 26: In New York, Mickey hits number 39.

August 2: In New York, Mickey hits number 40.

August 4: In New York, Roger hits number 41.

August 6: In New York, a doubleheader, Mickey hits three homers for number 43.

August 11: In D.C., M&M both hit homers: Mickey number 44, Roger number 42. Mickey's 44th "sailed deep into the bleachers in left-center."

August 12: In D.C., Roger hits number 43.

August 13: In D.C., a doubleheader, Maris "blast 2 homers, Mickey 1. Both have 45."

August 15: In New York, Roger hits number 46.

August 16: In New York, Roger hits numbers 47 and 48.

August 20: In Cleveland, Roger hits his 49th and Mickey hits his 46th.

August 22: In Los Angeles, Roger hits number 50.

August 27: In Kansas City, Roger hits number 51. August 30: In Minnesota, Mickey hits his 47th.

August 31: In Minnesota, Mickey hits number 48.

September 2: In New York, Roger hits numbers 52 and 53.

September 3: In New York, Mickey blasts numbers 49 and 50, the former soaring into the left-field bleachers.

September 5: In New York, Mickey hits number 51. September 6: In New York, Roger hits number 54. September 7: In New York, Roger hits number 55. September 8: In New York, Mickey blasts number 52. September 9: In New York, Roger hits number 56. September 10: In New York, Mickey hits number 53.

September 16: In Detroit, Roger "blasts his 57th off the roof of the second deck in right field."

September 17: In Detroit, Roger's 58th wins the game for the Yankees.

September 20: In Baltimore, Roger hits number 59.

September 23: In Boston, Mickey hits his 54th, Whitey earns his 25th win.

September 26: In New York, Roger hits number 60.

October 1: In New York, Roger hits number 61 off Tracy Stallard in the 162nd game.

October: Mickey has a bleeding abscess in his right hip and misses most of the World Series against the Reds.

October 7: In Cincinnati, Roger homers in the ninth inning for a Yankee winning hit. The Yankees go up 2 – 1 in games. Whitey sets the World Series record of 32 scoreless innings in a row.

October 9: The Yankees win the Series 4 – 1.

October 16: M&M named to the AL All-Star team by the Baseball Writers' Association of America.

November 15: Roger edges out Mickey for the MVP Award by four points. Roger led the league in home runs (61), RBIs (141), runs (132), and total bases (366); he also had .620 SLG and .269 BA. Mickey led the league in slugging percentage (.687), on-base percentage (206), and BB (126). For the season, he accumulated 54 home runs, 128 RBIs, and a BA of .317.

December 13: Mickey signs for $85,000; Roger holds out.

1962

January 22: Roger wins the Pro Athlete of the Year Award, the Hickok Belt, awarded in Rochester, New York.

February 26: Roger signs for $72,000.

March 10: In Ft. Lauderdale for spring training, Mickey hits a 420-foot home run.

March 15: In Ft. Lauderdale, hits a three-run homer that clears the 420-foot sign, the first at the new spring training facility.

March 26: Mickey hits a home run.

March 29: At Vero Beach, Mickey hits a homer. March 30: In Miami, Mickey hits a 425-foot "wallop."

April 10: In New York on Opening Day, "M&M clout homers. Mickey's goes into the right-center field bleachers."

April 14: In Detroit, Mickey "makes a shoestring catch to stop the Tigers' rally."

April 20: In Baltimore, Mickey hits a more-than 400-foot drive for a home run.

May 6: In New York, Mickey hits 3 home runs in a doubleheader, including a 450-foot drive that flies into the right-center bleachers.

May 18: "Injured left knee and right thigh puts Mickey out."

June 16: In first return since May 18th, hits a three-run, 450-foot homer in Cleveland.

June 28: In New York, M&M hit homers, including Mickey's 10th.

June 30: Mickey gets named to the All-Star team with the second-highest vote total.

July 2: In New York, M&M homer.

July 3: In New York, M&M both hit two homers.

July 4: In New York, Mickey hits two homers in the first game. Roger homers in the second game.

July 6: In Minnesota, M&M both hit two homers in one game. Mickey gains four homers in four consecutive at bats.

July 10: Mickey enters the All-Star game, hitting .333.

July 18: In Boston, Mickey drives in four runs.

July 25: In New York, Mickey hits a "blast into the upper right field deck."

August 19: In Kansas City, Mickey and Ellie Howard drive in 15 runs combined. Mickey played 6 innings: Grand Slam, double, single, two stolen bases, and 7 RBIs. Ellie drives in eight: two HRS, a triple, and a single.

September 4: Mickey has a rib injury.

September 10: In Detroit, returns and hits home run number 400 for his career, a "towering" 450-foot home run.

September 15: Mickey is named the Outstanding AL Player of the Year by Sporting News; Maury Wills named Outstanding Player in the NL.

September 30: Mickey scores home run number 30 and is hitting .321.

October 17: Named to the Major League All-Star team.

October 18: Wins his fourth Slugging crown with .624.

November 20: Mickey wins his third MVP Award and later the Gold Glove award.

1963

February 27: Mickey signs for $100,000, tying Joe DiMaggio for the highest Yankee salary ever. Babe Ruth made $80,000.

May 7: In Detroit, Mickey hits a sacrifice fly and a two-run homer to win

May 11: In Baltimore, M&M Boys hit homers and drove in three runs each.

May 21: In New York, Mickey "smashes" two homers and drives in five; Roger hits one.

May 22: "At Yankee Stadium, in the bottom of the 11th inning, facing right hander Bill Fischer of Kansas City, Mickey hits the longest homer in baseball ever. Mickey's (still) raising line-drive hit the facade of the roof above the right field deck. Mickey missed by about five feet, hitting the ball out of Yankee Stadium. The ball went well over 500 feet." Later estimates by qualified experts say that, unimpeded, the ball would have traveled 732, 734, or 740 feet.

June 6: In Baltimore, Mickey breaks a bone in his foot sliding into the center-field fence, going after a fly ball.

July 2: Named to the All-Star team and cannot play.

August 4: In New York, first appearance back; hits a pinch-hit home run.

September 1: In Baltimore, Mickey "hits a pinch-hit home run to ignite the Yankees rally."

September 12: In Kansas City, Mickey goes 3 – 4 with a homer and drives in four runs.

October 6: Mickey hits his 15th World Series home run, a 420-footer off Koufax, which ties him with Babe Ruth for career HRs. October: Yogi is named the Yankees Manager.

1964

February 27: Mickey signs for $100,000 after playing only 65 games in 1963. "Mantle is a tremendous asset to the Yankees and to baseball."

March 29: At spring training in Tampa, Mickey belts two homers.

May 6: In D.C., in a doubleheader, Mickey hits two homers, and Roger hits one.

May 16: In New York, Roger hits two homers, and Mickey hits one.

May 24: "Mickey homers in the second inning and ignites a four-run rally with a two-strike bunt in the sixth inning."

June 11: In Boston, Mickey hits two homers in a win. "The first, a towering drive into the bullpen in right field, at least 425 feet." Roger hits a homer.

June 12: In Boston, Mickey "smashes another into the right field bullpen." Mickey's average is .331.

June 21: Mickey is named to the All-Star team.

July 4: In New York, "belts number 17 into the third deck in right field" for a .333 BA.

July 20: Is posted as the RBI career leader in the AL, going into 1964, with 1,187.

August 1: In Minnesota, "Mickey powers the Yankees to victory" with a 420-foot homer and 400-foot double.

August 12: In New York, "Mickey slugs two homers, one tape-measured blast" over the 22-foot, five-inch-high screen in center field and above the 461-foot mark, off Herbert. "The ball lands 15 rows up in the stands. Only two balls were ever hit there. Mickey hit the other on June 21, 1955. This one was the longer of the two. Roger also hits a homer."

September 3: In Kansas City, Mickey hits number 30.

September 17: In New York, Mickey hits career homer number 450. September 19: In New York, Mickey hits two homers.

September 30: In New York, Mickey hits number 35.

October 10: In New York, "bombs" a ball off Barney Schultz, which hits the facade of the second deck in right field, securing a World Series win in the ninth inning. This home run places him as the all-time career leader, surpassing Babe Ruth.

October 14: Hits World Series homer number 17; Roger hits a homer, too. Mickey sets the bar for total World Series bases at 119 over Yogi's 117.

October 15: Hits homer number 18 off Bob Gibson. Mickey holds the World Series records for most Runs (42) and RBIs (40).

October: Mickey is named to the AP All-Star team. The Yankees fire Yogi after the Yankees lose in seven games. They hire an outsider Johnny Keane from St. Louis.

October 18: Mickey gathers the second-highest total for MVP, to Brooks Robinson. Mickey hits .303 (fourth), 35 homers, 111 RBIs, SLG .591 (second), OBS .423 (first), PPS 1.015 (first), 18 intentional walks (first), leading the league in the last three categories. Brooks hits 317 BA, 118 RBIs, SLG .521, OBP .363, and OPS .889, leading the league in RBIs.

1965

April 15: Mickey signs for $100,000 again.

April 17: In Kansas City, Mickey and Roger both hit two-run homers. "Roger's homer cleared both the inner in right field plus an outer wall that sits atop a 40-foot embankment. Only seven balls have been over the second wall."

April 21: In New York, Mickey hits a home run into the third tier of the right-field stands for number 457 in his career.

April 25: In New York, "Mickey helps the Yankees sweep Los Angeles. He homers in the second game for a 1 – 0 win."

May 15: In Baltimore, Mickey "clouts one into the left-field bleachers for a game-winning homer."

June 18: In New York, "belts a Grand Slam to trigger a Yankee win."

July 11: Scores his 1,500th run.

September 2: In Los Angeles, hits a three-run homer and drives in four. September 18: Plays his 2,000th game and gets honored at Yankee Stadium. He donates all proceeds to the Hodgkin's Disease Research Fund.

1966

March: Misses spring training due to shoulder surgery.

March 31: Does not play in the spring training game but during batting practice, "he hits 30 balls over the wall."

May 14: In Kansas City, hits career home run number 475.

May 25: In New York, hits two homers and drives in four.

June 28: In Boston, hits two home runs.

June 29: In Boston, hits two homers and drives in four.

July 2: In D.C., hits two home runs.

July 7: In New York, hits a three-run homer in the ninth to beat the Red Sox.

July 8: In New York, hits two homers in a doubleheader against the Senators, with one traveling 450 feet.

July 23: In New York, hits his ninth career Grand Slam.

July 24: In New York, hits number 493, tying him with Lou Gehrig.

July 29: In Detroit, hits number 494 into the second deck.

October 26: In New York, pinch-hit a two-run homer in the ninth inning, gives the Yankees a 6 – 5 win.

December: Mickey fields 1.000 for the year.

December 8: Roger gets traded to St. Louis.

1967

January 31: Mickey signs his $100,000 contract and "agrees to try playing first base."

April 29: In New York, hits his first homer of the season and 494th in his career.

April 3: In New York, hits a "towering" three-run home run in the 10th inning for a Yankees win, number 498.

May 2: Makes his first error in 133 games.

May 3: In Minnesota, hits number 499. May 14: In New York, hits number 500.

May 20: In Detroit, "clouts a homer off Denny McLain, high into the second deck."

May 22: In Detroit, hits his eighth homer of the year, four in four days.

June 5: In New York, beats Washington with an eighth-inning homer.

June 12: Mickey and Roberto Clemente are named the winners of the Van Heusen outstanding players for May. Mickey hits eight homers over a 13-game span.

June 15: In D.C., Mickey hits number 509, the game winner, into the second deck in left-center field.

June 24: In New York, Mickey's home run in the bottom of the ninth inning beats Detroit.

June 30: Named to the All-Star team. He has appeared in 14 and was named three other times. (For a few years, there was more than one game played.)

July 4: In Minnesota, hits homer number 15 and number 512 to pass Mel Ott on the all-time list. He now ranks fifth on the career home runs list.

July 16: In New York, hits number 513 into the right-center field bleachers.

September 2: In New York, pinch-hits a two-run homer in the eighth inning to beat Washington, 2 – 1.

September 21: "Mickey has won 15 games for the Yankees this year with crucial hits."

1968

February 27: Mickey signs his sixth consecutive contract for $100,000.

April 26: In New York, hits number 521 and ties Ted Williams for career homers.

May 30: In New York, goes five-for-five with two home runs and now has 524.

June 29: In New York, in a doubleheader against the A's and Reggie Jackson, Mickey has a homer in game one and drives in all five RBIs.

In game two, Mickey has an eighth-inning pinch-hit double for a 5 – 4 win and the sweep.

July 1: Named to the All-Star team for the 16th year and the 20th time.

September 10: In New York, hits two homers and now has 531.

September 12: In Minnesota, hits number 534, tying him with Jimmy Foxx for all time.

September 19: In Detroit, hits number 535 off Denny McLain and is third on the all-time career home run list.

September 20: In New York, hits number 536 off Jim Lonborg.

September 25: In New York, Mickey hits a "clean single," the only hit off Luis Tiant.

September 29: In New York, Mickey goes two-for-four in his last game.

1969

March 1: Mickey officially announces his retirement, after the baseball owners gave $500,000 into the MLBPA pension fund. Mickey played more games as any Yankee thus far: 2,401.

June 8: First official Mickey Mantle Day at Yankee Stadium.

1974

August 12: Mickey was inducted into the Baseball Hall of Fame on the first ballot. Whitey Ford was also inducted that day.

BIBLIOGRAPHY

A special thank-you goes out to Tim Wiles, the former Director of Research at the Baseball Hall of Fame, for allowing me (with white gloves) to research their players' files. Many joyful hours were spent there, particularly with the files of Mickey Mantle, Satchel Paige, and Pete Rose. A loud shout-out also goes to the Society for American Baseball Research (SABR).

Adair, Robert K. *The Physics of Baseball*. Harper & Row Publishers, Inc., 1990.

Alexander, Charles C. *John J. McGraw*. New York: Viking Penguin, Inc., 1988. Barra, Allen. *Yogi Berra: Eternal Yankee*. W.W. Norton & Company, 2010. Cobb, Ty, Al Stump, and Charles C. Alexander. *My Life in Baseball: The True Record*. UNP-Bison Books, 1993.

Cramer, Richard Ben. *Joe DiMaggio: The Hero's Life*. Simon & Schuster, 2000. Creamer, Robert W. *Babe*. New York: Simon & Schuster, Penguin Book Publishing, 1983.

Creamer, Robert W. *Stengel: His Life and Times*. New York: Fireside Books, 1989.

Dickson, Paul. *Baseball Dictionary*. New York: Facts on File, 1989. Donovan, Richard. "The Fabulous Satchel Paige." In *The Fireside Book of Baseball,* edited by Charles Einstein, 75-95. New York: Simon & Schuster, 1956.

Durocher, Leo, and Ed Linn. *Nice Guys Finish Last*. New York: Simon & Schuster, 1975.

Gallagher, Mark. *The Yankee Encyclopedia.* New York: Leisure Press, 1982. Golenbock, Peter. *Dynasty: The New York Yankees 1949-1964.* New York: Berkley Books, 1975.

Houk, Ralph, and Robert Creamer. *The Season of Glory.* New York: G.P. Putnam's Sons.

James, Bill. *The Politics of Glory.* New York: Macmillan Publishing Company, 1994.

Kahn, Roger. *Memories of Summer.* New York: Hook Slide, Inc., 1997. Kubek, Tony, and Terry Pluto. *Sixty-One.* New York: Macmillan, 1987.

Leavy, Jane. *The Last Boy, Mickey Mantle.* New York: Harper Collins, 2018.

Lebovitz, Hal. *Pitchin' Man.* Westport: Meckler Corp., 1992.

Leib, Fred. *Baseball as I Have Known It.* New York: Tempo Books, Grosset & Dunlap, 1977.

Macht, Norman L. *Satchel Paige.* New York: Chelsea House Publishing, 1991. McCarthy, John P. *Baseball's All Time Dream Team.* Cincinnati: Betterway Books, 1994.

Mantle, Mickey, and Herb Gluck. *The Mick.* New York: Jove/Doubleday & Co., 1985.

Miller, Marvin. *A Whole Different Ball Game.* New York: Birch Lane Press, 1994.

Montville, Leigh. *Ted Williams: The Biography of an American Hero.* New York: Doubleday, 2004.

Nelson, Kevin. *Baseball's Greatest Insults.* New York: Simon & Schuster, Inc., 1984.

Nuttall, David S. *Mickey Mantle's Greatest Hits.* New York: SPI Books, 1998.

Richardson, Bobby. *Impact Player.* Tindale House Publishers, 2012.

Ritter, Lawrence S. *The Glory of Their Times.* New York: A.S. Barnes and Co., 1984.

Schlossberg, Dan. *The Baseball Catalog.* Middle Village, New York: Jonathan David Publishers Inc., 1980.

Seymour, Harold. *The Golden Age.* Oxford University Press, 1971.

Silverman, Al. *Mickey Mantle Mister Yankee.* New York: G. P. Putnam's Sons, 1963.

Smith, Ken. *Baseball's Hall of Fame.* New York: Tempo Books/Grosset & Dunlap, 1979.

Sport Magazine's All-Time All Stars. Edited by Tom Murray. New York: Signet, 1977.

Susman, Paul E. "Mantle: All-Time King of the Tape-Measured Homers." *Baseball Digest,* June 1982.

Total Baseball, Fifth Edition: The Official Encyclopedia of Major League Baseball. Edited by John Thorn and Pete Palmer. New York: Viking, Penguin Books, 1997.

Underwood, John, and Ted William. *My Turn at Bat.* New York: Simon & Schuster, 1988.

Will, George. *Men at Work. The Craft of Baseball.* New York: Harper Perennial, 1990.

News and reports from: Associated Press *Baseball Digest Baseball Weekly*

The Chicago Daily

The Chicago Sun-Times

The Democrat and Chronicle Minneapolis Star Tribune MLB.com

Newsweek

The New York Times

Society for American Baseball Research (SABR)

SPORT Sporting News Sports Illustrated

Street & Smith's Baseball

The Rochester Times Union United Press International USA Today

ACKNOWLEDGEMENTS

A very sincere thanks goes out to my dear friends and family, who have been so supportive in this labor of love. I truly appreciate your time and efforts, wisdom and knowledge. I am certain that without all your assistance, this book would not be so complete and well-thought- out.

Special thanks to Gary Carter, Hank Bauer, Tommy John, Bob Mathias, Clete Boyer, Tim McCarver, Tim Wiles (formerly) of the National Baseball Hall of Fame, Scott Pitoniak, David Halberstam, Maurine and Lee Johnson, Lauren Kravetz Bonnet, Ben Bonnet, Chris Bonnet, Adam Kravetz, Ralph Hyman, Senator Rich Funke, Tom Murphy, James E. Williams, Gary "Bubba" Snyder, Paul Eggert, Robert Heinig, M.D., Coach George Steitz, Ken Slater, Norman E. Hurwitz, Garry Hurwitz, Mark Hurwitz, George Reiber, William E. Boden, M.D., Kerstin E. Nourse, Dave Lanning, and Sarah Motyka.

I also want to thank Paul E. Susman- his friends and associates, Johnny Blanchard, Lewis Early, Paul Richards, Sparky Anderson, Stan Musial, Tony Kubek, Max Mantle, Frankie Crosetti, Harmon Killebrew, Bill Dickey, Larry Napp, Joe Ginsberg, Mrs. Jackie Jensen, Maury Allen, Mike North, Clark Griffin, Bill Fischer, Rod Dedeaux, Robert Schiewe.

The largest thank-you goes to my dear wife Jill, for encouraging me to "play two."

"You just don't know"

"It aint over until it's over" –*Yogi*

And that is the exquisiteness of baseball. You just don't know. Let me illustrate this point with this very poignant vignette, told to me by my friend, Tim Wiles, former Director of research, Cooperstown Baseball Hall of Fame:

Most baseball buffs know about the most remarkable World Series. The 1905 Series was the one where the GREAT Christy Mathewson pitched 27 innings in starting three games (one on two days rest) and allowing ZERO earned runs. That is 0.00– just like Blutarski's GPA in *Animal House*. Matty pitched three shutouts and obviously won all three games. But just as amazing was that all five games of the Series were shutouts, with the Giants beating the Philadelphia A's 4-1 in games. (Chief Bender for N.Y. in Game 2 and McGinnity for the A's in Game 4.)

So, the Giants won the World Series, and "Big Six" Matty (who was also known as "Gun Boots" during his collegiate days at Bucknell) was the best pitcher in the world. Matty just went 32-8 for the season, including his second pseudo no-hitter, besides his astounding World Series performance. Giant's catcher Frank Bowerman was going home to celebrate in his hometown of Romeo, Michigan. He realized that his own local team was about to play for their hometown championship. Although he was a professional, he felt a real allegiance to his old team and announced that he would catch for them. Going one step further, because this game was for all the marbles and more importantly all the bragging rights, since he was going to catch, it was only logical that he should bring in his battery mate, Christy Mathewson, to pitch against these amateurs. Mathewson was brilliant in his own estimation. According to Matty, it was the only game that he ever pitched where he had complete concentration before each pitch and perfect mechanics of every single pitch he threw! His rhythm was perfect. He also put the ball exactly where he intended to, in terms of location. He never, ever pitched a game like that before or after. HE ALSO LOST 5-0!

ABOUT THE AUTHOR

Robert Kravetz fell in love with baseball as a boy in the 1950s and 1960s. A baseball historian, he is also the author of Where Have You Gone Mickey Mantle? He has supported various Little Leagues, Challenger Baseball, Children Awaiting Parents, and other worthy organizations that benefit children with book proceeds. When Gary Carter met the author in Rochester, New York, he was so delighted with his baseball stories that he wrote the foreword to Baby Boomer Baseball.